D1254954

Let's Knit!

 KALMBACH BOOKS

21027 Crossroads Circle
Waukesha, Wisconsin 53186
www.Kalmbach.com/books

© 2008 Monette Satterfield. All rights reserved. This book may not be reproduced in part or in whole without written permission of the publisher except for brief excerpts for review.

Published in 2008
12 11 10 09 08   1 2 3 4 5

Manufactured in the United States of America

ISBN: 978-0-87116-271-7

Publisher's Cataloging-in-Publication Data

Satterfield, Monette Lassiter.
   Let's knit! : the beginner's guide to knitting / by Monette Satterfield.

   p. : ill. ; cm.

   ISBN: 978-0-87116-271-7

1. Knitting--Technique. 2. Knitting--Patterns. I. Title.

TT820 .S28 2008
746.43/2

The **beginner's guide** to knitting

Let's Knit!

by Monette Satterfield

KALMBACH BOOKS

Contents

PROJECTS

WEARABLES

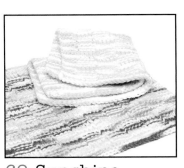

Why Learn to Knit?

There are so many reasons to learn to knit. Many people knit for pure enjoyment—they love the materials and find the rhythmic quality of knitting soothing and relaxing.

Other people enjoy the social aspect of knitting. Knitting and stitching groups are springing up all over the country, each with its own personality. These social ties are creating whole new communities—knitting groups, conferences, workshops, blogs, and forums. Some are in-the-flesh meetings at local yarn shops and coffee shops, while others are strictly online. The sense of community is strong, which is a good reason to join in!

Many others see the opportunity for personal expression as the most thrilling aspect of knitting. It's exciting to create your own garment or accessory that can't be found in any store. After all, anyone can buy something, but not everyone can make it. That brings me to my most compelling reason to knit: to celebrate the value of creating something with your own hands. Our world seems to be getting further away from the daily practice of doing actual things. If you knit, you know *how* to do something instead of just knowing *about* it.

HOW TO USE THIS BOOK

The patterns in this book are for beginners, so they are easy, fun, and can be customized. Many of the projects are great gifts for the same reasons.

Learning to knit is remarkably easy. There are only two stitches: knit and purl. Everything else is a variation on those two stitches. Starting with the first project in the book will get you started with knit stitches, and then you're on your way.

A note about the yarns used in this book: Despite their popularity, the fuzzy, furry, and fluffy novelty yarns are not used here. They are more difficult for beginners to work with because the stitches are hard to see. While you are learning to knit and purl, it's best to be able to see your stitches. Smoother worsted-weight yarns will help you do that.

The best way to learn to knit is to just get started. If you already know how to knit, or even knit and purl, feel free to pick any project that appeals to you. For a beginner, the scarf and hoodie are great projects, as well as the pot holder and washcloth. Just remember, knitting is NOT rocket science! People have knitted without written patterns for hundreds of years.

Once you get going on a project, refer to the Basic Techniques section if you need a little help. Also, don't be afraid to ask someone who knits; generally, knitters are a very helpful group, so just ask!

As for reference material, consider building your own personal library. Various books will come in handy as your skills develop and you take on more challenging projects. Authors explain methods differently, and you'll get a variety of valuable tips and viewpoints. Some suggestions to get you started are listed in Resources, p. 93.

LEARNING STYLE

We all learn differently. I like to read instructions and then try them myself. Some people prefer to be shown how to do something, and others need verbal explanations. Don't hesitate to ask a friend or try something different if the method you're using is not working.

ON A PERSONAL NOTE

I learned to knit as a young woman, newly married and fresh out of college. True to my read-and-try form, I learned on my own from a how-to booklet. I remember the first project I made from that leaflet—a pair of red and white garter-stitch slippers. I was thrilled!

Creative Options

At the end of each set of project instructions is a section called "Creative Options." These are suggestions to make the pattern differently from the basic instructions. I often look at a finished design and try to think of what else could be done to make it even more special. There are many ways to customize a pattern and make it yours— these are just a starting point.

There is not a rating system or difficulty level for the projects. The techniques used in the pattern are listed for each pattern. Check to see what techniques are required, and read through the pattern. If you're unsure about something, look it up in the Basic Techniques section and then proceed with confidence.

After that rousing success, I kept knitting and progressed to a simple sweater or two. That's when I learned the magic of designing your own projects. It was nothing more than simple math and a basic understanding of gauge. Again, I was thrilled!

Then I started designing my own simple pieces, and gradually progressed to more complex designs. During this time, I owned the local yarn store, which was another important learning experience for me. The shop is where I quickly learned how to teach the basics and troubleshoot other peoples' problematic knitting.

IN CONCLUSION

You will learn to knit from this book, of course, but more than that, I want you to have confidence in yourself and your knitting. You will make mistakes. We all have, and I know I'll make many more. I would be honored and proud for you to learn to knit here and go forward to make your mistakes and produce magnificent knitting.

Approach the whole undertaking with a spirit of adventure—it's just yarn, after all!

Getting Started

Materials & Tools

YARN

Ahhh, yarn—I could go on and on about how wonderful it is! Many types and qualities of yarn are available today.

Fiber

Fiber refers to the type of material from which yarns are made. Fibers fall into two categories: natural and synthetic. Natural fibers include animal fibers, such as wool, mohair, alpaca, cashmere, and silk, and vegetable fibers, such as cotton, linen, and ramie.

Many people learn to knit with wool. It is wonderfully forgiving and, in all but the hottest climates, comfortable to wear. Quality wool is one of the best fibers to use while learning how to knit. Wool is spun from sheep fleece and is available in many types and quality levels.

Types of Fibers

- **Wool** is warm, durable, and elastic. It also insulates against the cold and absorbs water well.
- **Mohair** is a warm, lightweight fiber made from the fleece of the Angora goat.
- **Alpaca** yarns are made from the shorn coat of the alpaca, a relative of the llama.
- **Angora** comes from the fur of Angora rabbits. It is very warm, soft, fluffy, and silky, but it may not stretch.

- **Cashmere** fibers are from the cashmere goat. Due to the tedious collection process, cashmere is one of the more expensive fibers.
- **Silk** is made from the filaments of silkworm cocoons. The fiber is very strong but not elastic.
- **Cotton** fibers come from the seed pod, or boll, of the cotton plant. It is absorbent and does not attract moths, but cotton yarns can be heavy and lack resilience.
- **Linen** fibers are derived from the stems of the flax plant. Like cotton, linen is very absorbent but lacks resilience. Usually linen is blended with other fibers to produce knitting yarns.

- **Rayon** is made of cellulose material that is synthetically constructed into fibers.
- **Bamboo** fiber is a popular new arrival to the knitting world. Often blended with other natural fibers, bamboo is lustrous, soft, and comfortable to wear.
- **Synthetic** fibers are generally easy to care for, durable, and inexpensive. There are a lot of finishes and types. Many of the fancy novelty yarns are synthetic fibers. Blends of synthetic fibers and natural fibers can produce a practical, beautiful yarn. Common synthetic fibers are nylon, acrylic, polyester, and viscose/rayon.

Three types of novelty yarn

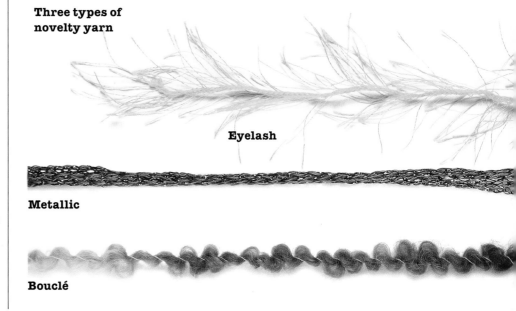

Eyelash

Metallic

Bouclé

Yarn Structure

Spinning is the basic method of making yarn from raw fibers. Yarn is composed of fibers twisted together.

Each strand of fiber is known as a **ply** and the yarn is made up of a number of plies spun together. The number of plies has nothing to do with the weight of the yarn, but it can affect how much loft the yarn has. **Loft** is the amount of air trapped in the yarn fibers themselves and between the strands that form the yarn. Garments made of high-loft yarn tend to be warm and hold their shape.

Four strands of fiber make up this 4-ply yarn.

Weight

Yarn is categorized by weight. This is not how much a ball of yarn actually weighs; it is a classification system that sorts yarns into categories based on how thick or thin they are. Each weight category corresponds to a particular range of stitch gauges and needle sizes.

The confusing part is that different countries, or even different needleworkers, may have different terms for the same yarn weight. The table below shows some terms used to refer to yarn weights and the average number of stockinette stitches (see p. 15) or single crochet stitches over 4 in. (10cm).

When choosing a pattern, pay attention to the yarn weight specified. Using a thicker yarn makes a project go quickly because there are fewer stitches per inch and row. Thicker yarns often produce a warmer fabric than thinner yarns because of loft. Using a thick yarn with a high loft produces a hefty, bulky fabric. A thinner yarn may not have the insulating loft of a bulky yarn, but using it will result in a light, manageable fabric.

You should also consider ply, or strand, which refers to the number of threads that have been twisted together to create the yarn. You can count the number of plies in most yarns by untwisting the end. Some novelty yarns consist of just one strand. The weight of the plied yarn is not related to the number of strands; it refers to the thickness of the individual strands.

Colors and Dye Lots

Most yarn is dyed in batches or dye lots, which can vary slightly. Be sure to buy enough yarn from the same dye lot to finish your project. Yarn from different dye lots may be noticeably different when worked into a garment. Besides, having extra yarn enhances your stash!

TIP: Stash is a word used in popular knitting terminology. It generally refers to yarn waiting to be made into projects or yarn purchased "just in case" because it was too special to pass up.

Many wondrous hand- and specialty-dyed yarns are available today. You can choose from luscious, no-two-are-alike hand-dyed yarns, or you can pick lovely machine-dyed yarns that make complicated patterns as you work. Be sure to purchase enough of these yarns to complete your project too, as a new dye lot or batch can look completely different from the original.

Weight	Type	Knit Gauge	Crochet Gauge	YS Symbol
Superfine	Sock	27–32 stitches	21–32 stitches	1 SUPER FINE
	Fingering			
	Baby			
Fine	Sport	23–26 stitches	16–20 stitches	2 FINE
	Baby			
Light	DK	21–24 stitches	12–17 stitches	3 LIGHT
	Light Worsted			
Medium	Worsted	16–20 stitches	11–14 stitches	4 MEDIUM
	Afghan			
	Aran			
Bulky	Chunky	12–15 stitches	8–11 stitches	5 BULKY
	Craft			
	Rug			
Super Bulky	Bulky	6–11 stitches	5–9 stitches	6 SUPER BULKY
	Roving			

Source: Craft Yarn Council of America, www.yarnstandards.com

Ball, Skein, or Hank?

Yarn is available in several forms, most commonly balls, skeins, and hanks. Balls are just what you think—yarn wound into round balls. The yarn is worked from the outside of the ball. Skeins are bundles of yarn, some of which are designed as pull skeins with a yarn end sticking out so you can work from the center. Hanks are loose lengths of yarn twisted into a package. To work with these, first wind the yarn into a ball.

There are different ways to turn a tangle-prone loop of yarn into a tidy ball. You can use a ball winder and a swift, an umbrella-like device that holds the skein and feeds the yarn to the winder while you turn a handle. Or you could carefully arrange the hank around the backs of one or two straight chairs and wind the ball by hand. Lastly, but most companionably, is to have a helper hold the hank looped over his or her arms while you wind the ball. Just be sure that your helper's arms don't get too tired!

Yarn is available in balls, skeins and hanks.

hank

ball

skein

Quantities

While every effort has been made to ensure the listed quantities are enough to make the projects, every knitter is different and may need more or less yarn. Also, any changes to the pattern (like adding length or a creative option) may change the amount of yarn needed. If the sample project shown used the entire amount of yarn, that is noted in the pattern. You may want to purchase more unless you like to take chances.

It's smart to get a little extra yarn and check to be sure the dye lots are all the same.

Choosing a Yarn

Here are some of the indicators of a quality yarn: It is well spun, has good color saturation, and feels appropriate for the fiber (the wool is not scratchy, and the acrylic is not stiff). It also passes an in-store durability test: Rub a strand firmly between two fingers and check for loose fibers and strand breakage.

Be sure the yarn will work for the project (strong acrylic for kids' sweaters, hand-washable wool for ladies' gloves). If you are sensitive to certain fibers, check the labels carefully and rub the ball or skein vigorously on the inside of your forearm. Any sign of redness or irritation should be a warning. Don't buy this yarn if the item will be worn next to your skin.

You may hear about a "yarn snob," a term used to describe someone who buys and uses only yarn from exclusive and expensive sources and

fibers. That doesn't apply to me! The yarns in this book were especially selected to showcase the wide range available. Quality is available at all price levels, and you must judge whether the yarn you choose is a good buy at that price.

Where to Buy Yarn

You can visit craft and hobby stores, go to a local yarn store, and even shop online. Each option has its positives and negatives. Buying in person allows you to feel the yarn, and it gives you a much better chance to evaluate the quality and suitability of your purchase. However, you are limited to the selection available. Online buying opens up many new yarn possibilities, but it keeps you from that important touch-and-feel experience.

CHOOSING AND USING A PATTERN

One of the best things about knitting for yourself is that you are in complete control of the item you make. You choose the yarn, the fit, and the finishing details.

To make these decisions, consider some important points. First, think about color: Which tones are most flattering for you? Don't make the mistake of buying a yarn because it was a wonderful fiber in the wrong color. You'll wind up not wearing whatever you make because it doesn't suit you. Likewise, don't get caught up in bargain fever—there's a reason 15 balls of merino wool in an unusual color are half price. Don't fall for it!

Next, consider what it is about similar items you have that you like and dislike. If you don't like oversized shapes, you won't wear a bubble sweater, no matter how trendy it is. The same goes for more subtle details, like a crew neck rather than a V-neck, or a cardigan instead of a pullover.

Note your preferences for fibers. You may prefer cotton and blends to wool. Your climate may not be suitable for all wool, all the time. If you are indoors most of the time, you may not need a big, bulky Icelandic wool sweater, no matter how much fun it might be to knit.

Wear What You Like!

I prefer sweaters without ribbing at the sleeves and bottom, and I like to wear cardigans instead of pullovers. I just don't seem to wear vests, no matter how appealing they are. I made three or four of them before I realized that!

Fit

Pattern instructions usually offer a range of sizes, which are listed as a measurement in inches or centimeters or as S, M, L, etc. Be sure to compare your actual measurements to the finished size to ensure the item will fit properly. When you make a size that corresponds to your actual measurements, the finished item will be larger by a few inches. This amount is the wearing and design ease built into the pattern, and it can range from a slightly negative number, which would be a skin-tight garment, to as much as 8 in. (20cm) larger than the body inside.

When choosing the size to make, compare your own measurements to the finished size listed in the pattern, and consider the amount of ease allowed. Standard fitting

garments allow for about 4 in. (10cm) of ease. Don't be tempted to drastically reduce or eliminate the ease, or the garment may not fit.

Reading the Pattern

At first glance, the pattern may look as if it were written in some other language. However, there is logic to it. The abbreviations are generally standard and listed in the pattern, and the instructions go step by step.

First, sit down and read the entire pattern so you can check any unfamiliar abbreviations and make sure you understand the construction order and method. If there are multiple sizes, mark the size you want throughout the pattern to avoid confusion later. Consider the techniques used, and look up or practice anything unfamiliar to you.

Parentheses indicate multiple sizes or the repetition of a sequence of stitches. Watch for parentheses in your pattern, and mark them. Asterisks serve the same purpose. They can also refer you to an earlier portion of the instructions that needs to be repeated.

Charts

Directions for stitch patterns are often shown in two different ways: in written form and in charts. Written instructions tell you what to do with the stitches in each row

SAMPLE CHART:
Elongated Rib Check

☐ knit on right side rows, purl on wrong side rows

☐ purl on right side rows, knit on wrong side rows

Each box across represents a stitch; horizontal rows of boxes represent rows of stitches.

12 row repeat

4 stitch repeat

as you come to them. A chart shows a picture of each stitch and how it's worked. Some people prefer written instructions, and others like to use charts. It is a personal preference, and neither way is "right." Some patterns offer both forms, especially difficult and complex patterns. It is helpful to be familiar with both written instructions and charts, as patterns may be easier to follow in one format or the other.

Charts use a square to represent each stitch and a symbol inside the square to indicate how to work the stitch. While the symbols vary somewhat, they are becoming more standardized. Each chart also has a key to reading it. Begin by reviewing the chart key. Generally, if the first row is a right-side row, charts start in the bottom right-hand corner and read from right to left. The second row is read from left to right.

Charts represent the pattern of the knitted fabric from the right side only. This means that on wrong-side rows (from left to right), you should purl any stitch that has a knit symbol and knit any stitch that has a purl symbol (see p. 21). If you're knitting in the round, follow the chart without worrying about whether you have the wrong or right side of the fabric facing.

Usually not all of the stitches are represented. To avoid overly large charts, the stitch "repeat" is usually sectioned off. This just means to repeat that section over and over again. The right-side (RS) rows are read from right to left, but the wrong-side (WS) rows are read from left to right. Some patterns may begin on a RS row, and others may begin on a WS row. Often, arrows indicate the knitting direction and remind you what direction to read the chart (and whether it's a RS or WS row).

ABBREVIATIONS

There are many commonly used abbreviations in knitting patterns. Some of these abbreviations are not used in this book, but they are good to know when you move on to other knitting projects.

[ ]: work instructions within brackets as many times as directed

( ): work instructions within parentheses in the place directed

* *: repeat instructions following the asterisks as directed

*: repeat instructions following the single asterisk as directed

alt: alternate

approx: approximately

beg: begin/beginning

bet: between

BO: bind off

CC: contrasting color

cm: centimeter(s)

cn: cable needle

CO: cast on

cont: continue/continuing

dec(s): decrease(s)/decreasing

dpn: double-pointed needle(s)

fl: front loop(s)

foll: follow/follows/following

g: gram(s)

inc: increase(s)/increasing

k: knit

k2tog: knit two stitches together

kwise: knitwise

LH: left-hand

lp(s): loop(s)

m: meter(s)

MC: main color

mm: millimeter(s)

M: make one; increase

oz: ounce(s)

p: purl

p2tog: purl two stitches together

patt(s): pattern(s)

pm: place marker

prev: previous

psso: pass slipped stitch over

pwise: purlwise

rem: remain/remaining

rep: repeat(s)/repeating

rev St st: reverse stockinette stitch

RH: right-hand

rnd(s): round(s)

RS: right side

sk: skip

sk2p: slip one, knit two together, pass slip stitch over the knit two together; two stitches have been decreased

skp: slip, knit, pass stitch over; one stitch has been decreased

sl: slip

sl1k: slip one knitwise

sl1p: slip one purlwise

sl st: slip stitch(es)

sm: slip marker

ssk: slip, slip, knit these two stitches together; a decrease

sssk: slip, slip, slip, knit three stitches together

st(s): stitch(es)

St st: stockinette/stocking stitch

tbl: through back loop

tog: together

WS: wrong side

wyb: with yarn in back

wyf: with yarn in front

yd(s): yard(s)

yfwd: yarn forward

yo: yarn over

yon: yarn over needle

yrn: yarn around needle

Stitch Patterns

Stitch patterns are based on repeats of stitches and rows. The stitch sequence repeats across a row, and a series of rows of those stitch sequences repeats vertically. Together they make up a stitch pattern that determines how your knits will look.

Stitch pattern instructions may begin by giving you a multiple of stitches that make a complete repeat of the pattern. Sometimes you need to work an extra stitch or two to make a specific pattern work. When you make a gauge swatch, cast on a multiple of the number plus the extra stitch(es) required. For example, if the pattern calls for a multiple of two stitches plus one, you could cast on 11 (2 x 5 + 1) stitches, 7 (2 x 3 + 1) stitches, or another similar calculation.

Gauge

Achieving the correct gauge is the key to knitting pieces the correct size. Gauge is the number of stitches and rows per inch, including fractions of stitches. Gauge is crucial for any item that must fit properly. Most knitting patterns include a recommended gauge. The patterns in this book list

how to make the gauge swatch and what its measurements should be. For some projects, such as scarves or pot holders, the exact gauge is not as crucial, and that is noted.

Gauge depends on many things: the yarn, the size of your tools, the pattern stitch used, and even how you feel that day! The gauge can also vary from color to color. For example, black yarn can work much differently than lighter colors of the same brand and type. The type of needle you choose also affects the gauge. You may obtain a slightly different gauge using aluminum tools than you would with wood or plastic. Yarn substitutions affect gauge too, since a different yarn may not work to the same gauge. You can still substitute yarns, but you must work a gauge swatch and adjust your needle size as needed. The projects in this book include recommendations for substituting yarn, but there is no substitute for creating a gauge swatch to make sure your yarn will work.

The gauge you obtain is unique to you. No matter what the pattern and yarn label say, check your gauge for every project with the needles you are going to use, even if you have used the same yarn before.

A different gauge will result in an item that is too large or too small.

Make a Gauge Swatch

To work a gauge swatch, knit a 4 in. (10cm) square in the pattern stitch with the yarn chosen and the needle size noted in the pattern. If you plan to launder your finished item, wash the swatch in the same manner. And if you are blocking the project pieces (see p. 26), block the swatch as well.

Lay the swatch flat, and count the stitches and rows in a 2-in. (5cm) square section of the swatch. Be sure to include fractions of stitches, because they can make a significant difference in the finished item.

Many patterns and yarn labels list gauge as a number of stitches per 4 in. (10cm). To convert your figures, multiply your stitch and row count by two and compare your gauge to that in the pattern for the 4-in. (10cm) swatch. If you have fewer stitches than the pattern requires, switch to smaller needles and work another gauge swatch. If your work has more stitches than required, try larger needles.

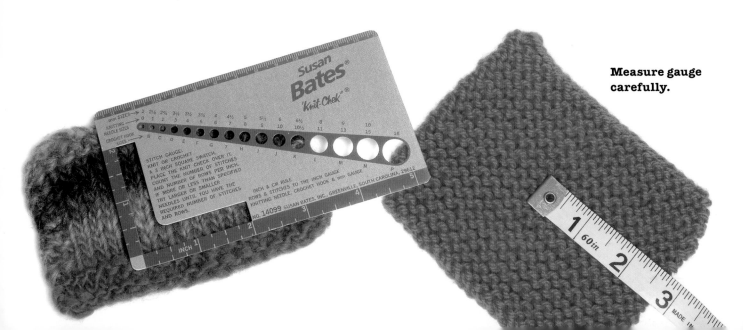

Measure gauge carefully.

COMMON STITCH PATTERNS

| | knit on right side rows, purl on wrong side rows | | purl on right side rows, knit on wrong side rows |

Garter stitch: Garter stitches are formed by working all stitches as knit stitches across every row (or as all purl stitches).

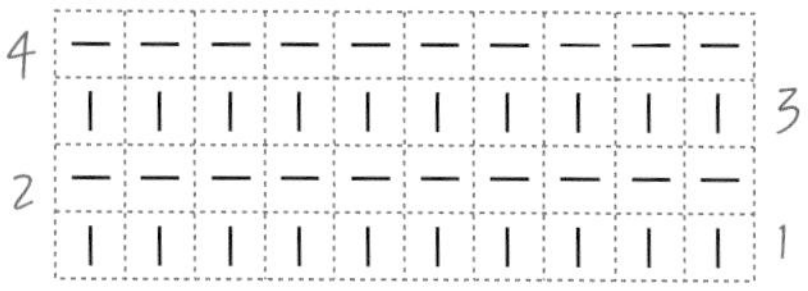

Stockinette stitch (St st): Work one row of knit stitches and one row of purl stitches; continue to alternate these rows. This stitch is widely used in knitting because it forms a smooth, flexible fabric.

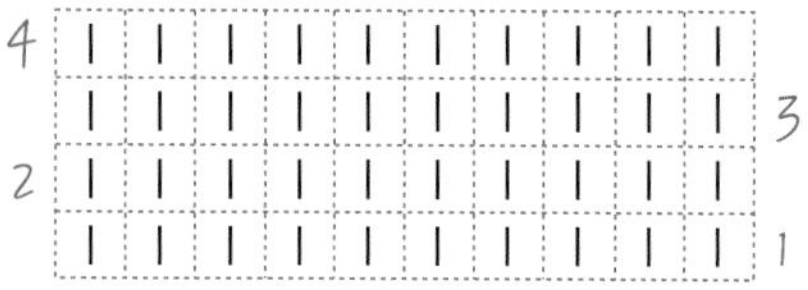

Reverse stockinette stitch: This is simply stockinette stitch with the purl side used as the right side of the work.

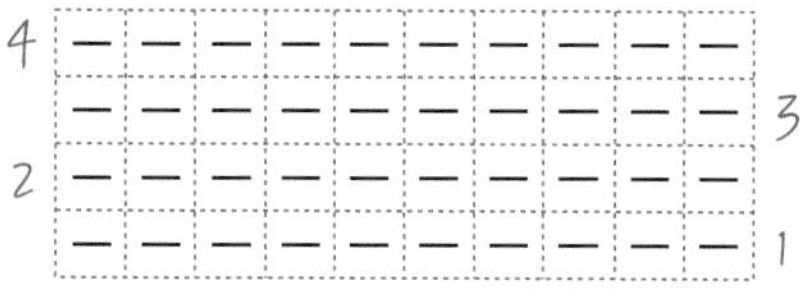

Seed stitch: This stitch is often used for borders and textural effects. It lies flat and looks the same on both sides. It is a knit 1, purl 1 ribbing broken on every row, so that a knit stitch is worked above every purl stitch and a purl is worked over every knit.

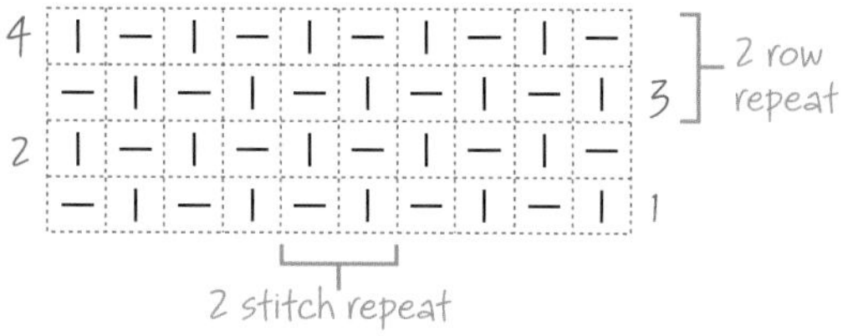

2 row repeat

2 stitch repeat

Moss stitch: This is another broken rib pattern, which gives a bolder texture than seed stitch. It is knit 1, purl 1 ribbing broken every other row.

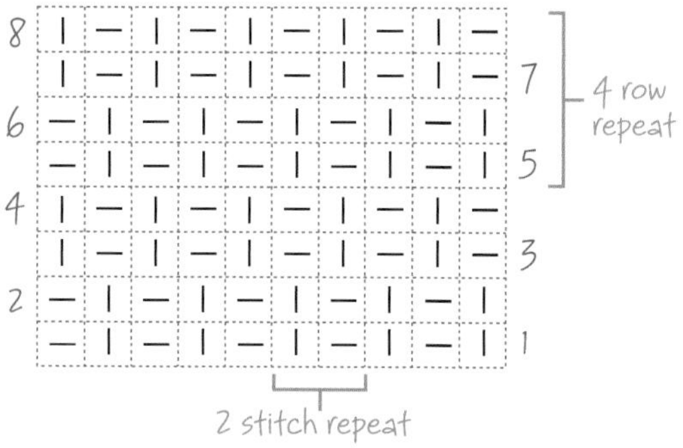

4 row repeat

2 stitch repeat

Ribbing 1 x 1: The simplest ribbing, it is very often used for sweater bands, cuffs, and neckbands.

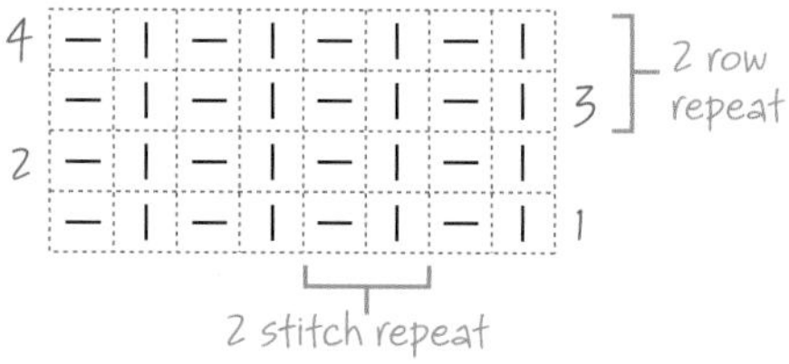

2 row repeat

2 stitch repeat

Ribbing 2 x 2: This is another very popular ribbing, but it does not pull in as much as knit 1, purl 1 ribbing.

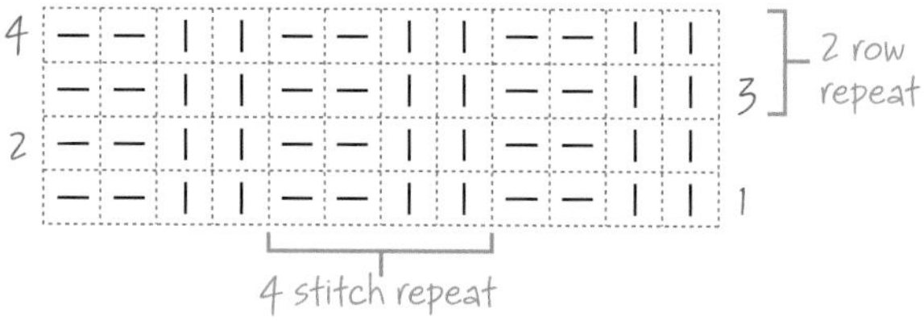

2 row repeat

4 stitch repeat

TOOLS AND EQUIPMENT

Needles

Knitting needles are available in a wide range of materials from natural to artificial. Natural materials include bamboo, wood, and even bone (although bone needles usually are antique and very hard to find). Metal tools can be aluminum (the most common) or steel, which can rust. Artificial materials include plastic, glass, and some of the new resin compounds. If you are just starting out, bamboo knitting needles are a good choice because bamboo needles have traction and the stitches are easy to control.

As you gain experience, be sure to try different needle materials and brands. All needles work a little differently; some may work better with certain yarns or just feel nicer in your hands.

Straight Needles

These are the needles that everyone pictures when they think about knitting. They come in pairs ranging from very fine size 0 (2mm) to size 19 (15mm). They are available in different lengths as well; the most common length is 14 in. (36cm).

Circular Needles

Circular knitting needles are composed of two shorter-than-usual needles joined by a flexible cable. With circular needles, you can work in the round to make hats, socks, and sleeves. You can also use circular needles as you would a set of single-pointed needles, and then turn the work at the end of the row and switch the needles in your hands. They allow the weight of the knitting to rest in your lap to reduce the strain on your hands, they are easier to tuck away neatly, and, because they are connected, you

probably won't lose just one!

Circular needles come in lengths ranging from 11½ in. (29cm), which are for very small areas such as socks or cuffs, to 16, 24, 29, and 36 in. (41, 61, 74, and 91cm). The actual length depends on the manufacturer. Some manufacturers produce needles up to 60 in. (1.5m) long. When choosing a needle, select the shortest length that will hold all of the stitches comfortably. A needle that is too long is just as frustrating as one that is too short.

Double-pointed Needles

Double-pointed needles are an alternative to circular needles for knitting in the round. Buy double-pointed needles in sets of four or five. Use them to make knitted cord as well.

KNITTING NEEDLE SIZES

Millimeter (mm)	2.0	2.25	2.75	3.25	3.5	3.75	4	4.5	5	5.5	6	6.5	8	9	10	12.75	15	19	25
U.S. size	0	1	2	3	4	5	6	7	8	9	10	10½	11	13	15	17	19	35	50

circular needles

straight needles

double-pointed needles

Accessories

There are many different knitting accessories available, and searching for the perfect tool can be fun! Here are some examples:

- **Tape measure:** Buy a good-quality tape measure. Replace it occasionally, as it can stretch with use and become inaccurate.
- **Stitch/needle gauge:** Use gauges to measure your swatches and identify the size of your unlabeled needles.
- **Stitch marker rings:** Stitch marker rings come as split, plain, and locking rings made of plastic or metal. Slip marker rings onto your needles to mark stitches, or place them into the knitting itself to mark specific rows.
- **Stitch holders:** These are useful for holding working stitches temporarily. You can also use a length of yarn or a circular needle with point protectors on the ends.

- **Point protectors:** Protectors keep stitches from falling off the needles while being transported.
- **Yarn needles:** These needles have large eyes and blunt tips for weaving in ends, sewing seams, and attaching and finishing items.
- **Scissors:** Choose a small, sharp pair for cutting yarn.
- **Plastic head or T-pins:** Pins with large plastic heads help to hold knitted pieces together as you sew. The large heads are clearly visible in the work.
- **Storage and project bags:** You'll need a handy container for storing your project. It could be a bag with a zipper or a designer tote.
- **Other accessories:** There are plenty of other items you may need or want. Browse the accessory department of your local store or look online for the latest can't-do-without gadgets.
- **Cable needles and bobbins:** These accessories are used for

more advanced techniques like cables and intarsia. Explore more accessories when you have mastered the basics!

For Beginners

If you are just starting, you don't need too many accessories. A basic set of tools will cover just about all situations:

- A small, sharp pair of scissors
- A good-quality measuring tape, retractable or not as you prefer
- Plain-ring and split-ring stitch markers
- A couple of small stitch holders
- A few yarn or tapestry needles
- Plenty of pins
- A set of point protectors

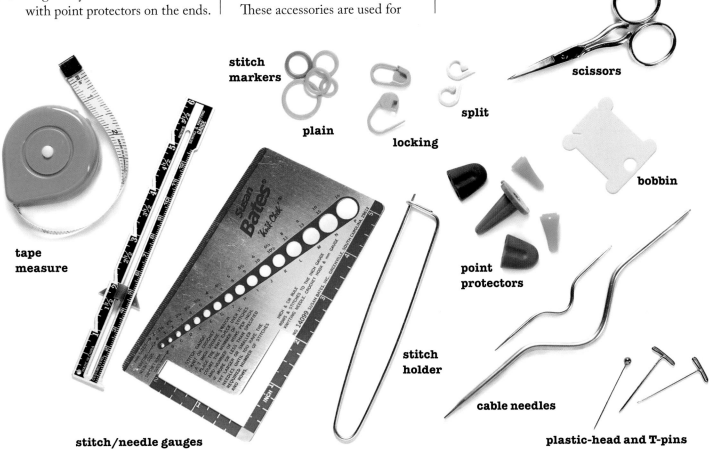

yarn needles

scissors

stitch markers

plain

locking

split

bobbin

tape measure

point protectors

stitch/needle gauges

stitch holder

cable needles

plastic-head and T-pins

Getting Started

Basic Techniques

ESSENTIALS

Holding the Yarn and Needles

There are many different ways to hold yarn and knitting needles. The most important thing is that you are comfortable and able to produce a result that satisfies you. The way you hold your yarn and needles will be a product of how you choose, or have learned, to knit. It is as individual as you are.

The two basic methods of holding the work are the English method and the Continental method. In the English method, you hold the working yarn (the ball of yarn) in your right hand. With the Continental method, the working yarn is held in your left hand. If you try one method but have trouble getting comfortable with your knitting or regulating the tension on the stitches, you can try the other method to see if it feels better.

Casting On

You must first cast on to begin to knit. Casting on creates a series of stitches on one needle that forms the edge of your knitting. There are quite a few different methods of casting on, and most knitters have their favorite.

The first cast-on technique on the next page is one that many knitters use because it is the easiest to master. It is often referred to as "knitting-on," as it is almost identical to the knit stitch itself. The second method presented is very similar but produces a much more attractive and sturdy edge. It is one of my favorite cast-on methods, and it is often called "cable cast-on." Give them both a try, and see which method you prefer.

English vs. Continental

Because the Continental method of holding the working yarn is similar to that used in crochet, you may find it much easier to master if you learn to crochet before learning to knit. I learned the English method first, and I did not really begin to enjoy knitting until I switched to the Continental method. Because of my crochet experience, it seemed to be a more natural way to hold the yarn.

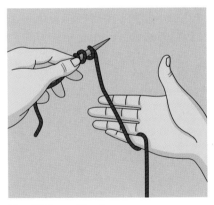

English method

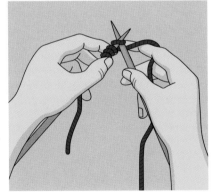

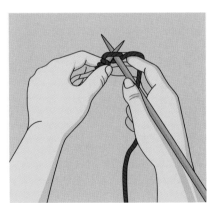

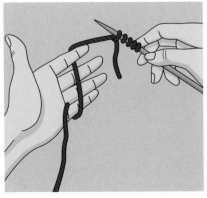

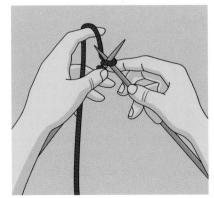

Continental method

Knitting-on

1 Pull the yarn end from the center of the skein and make a loop as shown, leaving a 6-in. (15cm) tail.

2 Insert the needle into the loop as shown. Pull the ball end of the yarn to tighten the loop around your needle and create a slipknot. This counts as your first stitch.

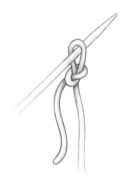

3 Hold the needle with the first stitch in your left hand, keeping the tail in front of the needle and the yarn from the skein in back of the needle.

4 Hold the empty needle in your right hand and slide its tip through the stitch on the left needle from left to right (from the front of the stitch to the back). The needles will form an X, with the right needle behind the left needle.

5 Hold the crossed needles between your left thumb and forefinger. Wrap the yarn from the skein counterclockwise around the tip of the right needle. Pull the tip of the right needle down and through the stitch, pulling the new loop through.

6 Gently stretch the loop on the right needle.

7 Working from left to right, slide the tip of the left needle through the loop on the right needle as shown.

8 Slide the right needle out of the loop, leaving two loops on the left needle. Pull gently to tighten the second stitch. Slide the tip of the right needle into the top stitch. Repeat steps 5–8 until you have cast on the required number of stitches.

Cable Cast-on

Follow steps 1–8 of the knitting-on cast-on once. You now have two stitches on the left needle.

1 Insert the right needle between the two stitches on the left needle, as shown.

2 Wrap the yarn from the skein counterclockwise around the tip of the right needle. Pull the tip of the right needle down and through the stitch, pulling the new loop through. Gently stretch the loop on the right needle.

3 Place the new stitch on the left needle as shown. Repeat steps 1–3 until you have cast on the required number of stitches.

TIP: The most common problem with a cast-on edge is stitches that are too tight so that the edge does not wear well. If your cast-on stitches are too snug, try making them with a needle that is one or even two sizes larger.

Knitting

The knit stitch is one of two fundamental stitches in knitting. To knit a stitch, you will use the right needle to pull a loop of yarn toward you through the stitch on the left needle, then move the stitch on the left needle to the end, and drop it off.

1 Hold the needle with the cast-on stitches in your left hand, with the first stitch (the last cast-on stitch) about 1 in. (2.5cm) from the needle tip. Slide the tip of the right needle into the first stitch, forming an X with the needles. Wrap the yarn from the skein counterclockwise around the tip of the right needle.

2 Slide the right needle and its loop down toward you, under the left needle and through the middle of the stitch.

3 Slide the stitch off the left needle, leaving the loop on the right needle. Repeat steps 1–3 until all of the stitches have been knit off the left needle; this completes your first row. Switch the empty needle to your right hand and the full one to your left hand and continue working rows.

Purling

The purl stitch is the second basic stitch you need to produce knitted fabric, and it is the reverse side of the knit stitch. When purling a stitch, the right needle pulls a loop of yarn through the stitches on the left needle just as in knitting. The difference is that you hold the working yarn in front of the needles instead of behind them.

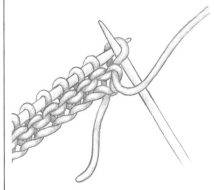

1 With the yarn in front of the left needle, insert the tip of the right needle from right to left into the stitch on the left needle. The right needle is in front of the left needle.

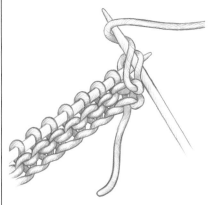

2 Wrap the yarn counterclockwise around the tip of the right needle.

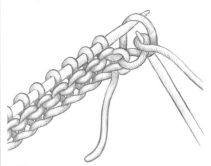

3 Slide the tip of the right needle along with the wrapped yarn back through the stitch away from you.

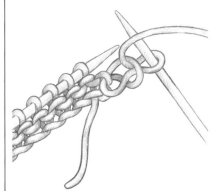

4 Slide the original stitch off the left needle, leaving the new stitch on the right needle. Repeat step 1–3 for each stitch on the left needle. Be sure the yarn is in front of the needles before you purl each stitch.

Increasing

Increasing means adding more stitches to a row. There are many different types of increases, and some are more visible than others. Two methods are used in the projects. The first, a visible increase, is called a bar increase because a horizontal bar will follow the increased stitch on the knit side. The second is a make-one increase. It is nearly invisible and is made by lifting a loop up from the previous row.

Bar increase (inc)

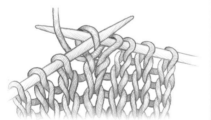

1 To add a knit stitch, slide the right needle into the stitch, wrap the yarn around the needle, and pull the loop down through the middle of the stitch. Do not drop the stitch off the left needle.

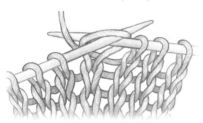

2 Bring the right needle to the back of the loop, and knit into it, dropping the loop off the needle when finished.

Yarn-over increase (inc)

A yarn-over is an increase that creates a lacy hole in the fabric for decorative effect. To make a yarn-over, wrap the yarn over the needle away from you. Continue to work the remaining stitches. There is now an extra loop on the needle that you work into as a stitch on the next row, being careful not to drop it before it's worked. To make a yarn over when purling, wrap the yarn over the needle from front to back and bring it back to the front. Continue purling the remaining stitches.

Make one (inc)

1 Insert the left needle from back to front into the horizontal strand in the row below. It is between the stitches you are currently working.

2 Knit this strand through the front loop to twist the stitch. If it is not twisted, a hole will appear in your work.

Decreasing

Decreasing is reducing the number of stitches in a row. As with increases, there are quite a few different types of decreases. Generally, your pattern will specify which type to use. If not, the simplest method is to knit or purl two stitches together (k2tog or p2tog).

Decrease (dec)

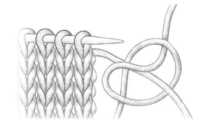

• Insert the right needle from front to back through two stitches on the left needle, and knit the stitches together. Or, insert the right needle from back to front through two stitches and purl together.

Joining New Yarn

Use this technique to add a new ball of yarn when the previous ball is used up or when joining another color when knitting stripes. Avoid joining in a new ball halfway through a row, if possible.

1 Tie the new yarn around the end of the old yarn, leaving a tail of at least 6 in. (15cm).

2 Move the knot close to the edge of the work, and begin the next row with the new yarn. When the work is complete, untie the knot and weave the ends in.

Binding Off

Binding off is the most common method of securing the stitches on a finished item. It links the stitches together so they don't unravel. The bound-off edge may be worked all the way across a piece, or groups of stitches may be bound off at different times to shape the work.

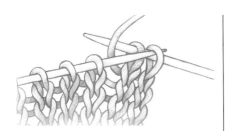

1 To bind off, place the full needle in your left hand and the empty needle in your right hand. Knit two stitches onto the right needle.

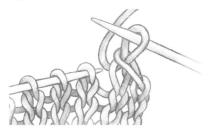

2 Slide the tip of the left needle into the first or outer stitch on the right needle, pull it up and over the second or inner stitch, and drop it off the needle.

3 This leaves one loop on the right needle. To continue, knit another stitch onto the right needle and repeat step 2.

4 When you reach the last stitch on the left needle, knit it onto the right needle and repeat step 2. One loop remains on the needle. Cut the yarn, remove the loop, pass the yarn through the loop, and tighten.

TIP: Bound-off edges can be too tight, especially a neck edge that stretches to go over your head. As with casting on, change to needles a few sizes larger than the work.

TIP: When binding off a specific number of stitches, count the stitches as you lift them off, not as you work them. The stitch remaining on the right-hand needle becomes the first stitch of the next row.

Weaving in Ends

Once all stitches have been bound off, weave the yarn ends in for a neat finish. Leave yourself at least 6 in. (15cm) of yarn so the ends are long enough to weave in properly. Don't cut the ends short or rely on a knot, as they can work loose and start unraveling. You can even leave extra-long ends to use for making seams.

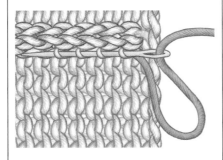

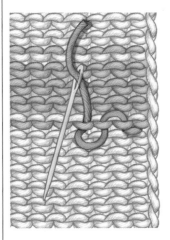

1 Thread the remaining yarn through a tapestry needle and weave it in and out of the purl bumps of a WS row for at least 2 in. (5cm) or along a seam edge. If possible, thread the ends into the same color work. Be careful not to pull so tightly that the fabric puckers.

2 Check the right side to see if the end shows and trim the excess yarn when finished.

OTHER BASIC TECHNIQUES

Picking up Stitches

This is the "pick-up-and-knit" technique that is often included as part of the finishing instructions for an item. It is used to begin working a section such as a neck band or border directly from the edge of a piece of knitting, thus avoiding having to cast on another piece and then join it with a seam. Another advantage is that the join is more elastic and less bulky than a seam. It is often more unobtrusive as well.

- To pick up stitches from the side of a piece, slide your right needle between the bars along the back side of the edge, wrap the yarn around the needle, and pull it through. Continue, spacing stitches evenly, until you have picked up the required amount of stitches. Alternatively, you can use a crochet hook to pull the loops through before placing them on the needle.

TIP: Space stitches evenly to create an attractive edge. Try doing it this way: Lay the work on a flat surface, divide it roughly into four sections, and mark with pins or markers. Divide the number of stitches to pick up by four, and pick up the resulting number from each section.

TIP: To pick up stitches on a cast-on or cast-off edge (the top or bottom), pick up one stitch in each stitch of the edge. To pick up along rows (the sides), pick up two stitches for every three rows or three stitches for every four rows, depending on the gauge of the project. As with all guidelines, use common sense here, as your situation may vary.

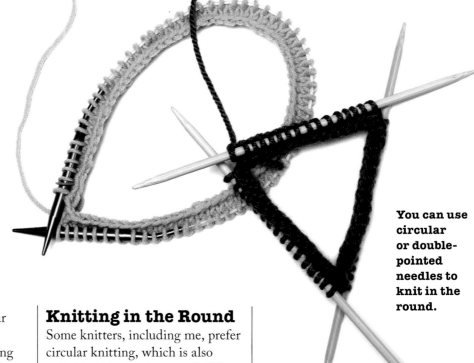

You can use circular or double-pointed needles to knit in the round.

Circular Knitting

Some people think that circular knitting is not a beginner technique, but this basic knitting skill looks more difficult than it really is. Go ahead and learn it now, while all knitting is new to you, so you won't put it off and become intimidated later!

Circular knitting needles have several advantages in addition to enabling you to work in the round. Use them to knit flat instead of using straight needles; just turn the work at the end of the row. This shifts the weight of the knitting to your lap, reducing the strain on your hands. Circular needles also are more portable. They never leave the knitting, so you won't lose a needle, and they tuck away more neatly than long, straight needles.

Circular needles come in a range of lengths, starting with 11½-in. (29cm) needles designed for very small pieces, such as socks or cuffs. (In some cases, circular needles are so awkward that using double-pointed needles may be easier.) Longer lengths include 16, 24, 29, and 36 in. (41, 61, 73.6, and 90cm). Some manufacturers even produce 60-in. (1.5m) circulars.

When choosing a circular needle, pick the shortest length that will still hold all of the stitches. A needle that is too long is just as difficult to work with as one that is too short.

Knitting in the Round

Some knitters, including me, prefer circular knitting, which is also called knitting in the round. When working in the round, the right side of the work is always facing you, so you work only right-side rows. In stockinette fabric, this means always working the knit stitch. (I don't know too many knitters who prefer purling to knitting, so this is a big advantage to working in the round.) The resulting fabric is smooth stockinette, not bumpy garter stitch. This little touch of knitting magic results from the construction of knit and purl stitches themselves. In effect, you work both the right-and wrong-side rows at the same time. (You can work garter stitch in the round by purling every other row.)

Circular knitting also reduces, or even eliminates, the need for sewing up seams, thus making finishing much easier. Most, but not all, stitch patterns can be worked in the round.

To knit in the round, use either a circular needle, which is two knitting needles joined by a flexible cable, or a set of double-pointed needles. With either method, you must make absolutely sure that the cast-on row is not twisted when you join to work in the round. A twisted cast-on row can't be fixed once you have worked past the first round. You will have to rip out the work and start over, so please check carefully!

Working with Circular Needles

1 Cast on as you normally would, and distribute the stitches around the needle, being sure not to twist them. Hold the needle with the last cast-on stitch in your right hand and the tip with the first cast-on stitch in your left. (You may wish to place a stitch marker to mark the beginning of the round.) Knit the first cast-on stitch, pulling the yarn snug to avoid a gap.

2 Continue to knit the cast-on row until you reach the beginning of the round. Double-check that the work is not twisted. You can still correct it at this point, as a small twist in one row will not

show. Continue working in the round, moving the stitch marker as needed.

Double-pointed Needles

While these may not be for everyone, they are worth a try. After all, nothing says "I know how to knit" like working a project on double-pointed needles.

These are the original needles for working in the round, and they still work well today. The principle is the same as for working on a circular needle; it just takes some practice to get used to working with more than two needles.

When using double-pointed needles, divide the stitches evenly among three or four needles (with one needle left to work the stitches). The more stitches to work, the more needles you will need.

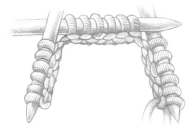

1 Cast on the required number of stitches. Arrange the needles with the cast-on edge toward the center.

2 Hold the needle with the last cast-on stitch in your right hand and the needle with the first cast-on stitch in your left. Knit the first cast-on stitch, pulling the

yarn snug to avoid a gap. Continue to work across the first needle. When all stitches are worked off, it becomes the free needle. Using the free needle, work across the next set of stitches. Continue working in rounds in this manner.

Dropped Stitches

Dropped stitches are also known as mistakes. Everybody makes them from time to time, and it's important to know how to fix them. Lay your work out occasionally and take a good look at it to spot any problems. Mistakes are easier to correct the sooner they are found.

A dropped stitch is just that—a stitch that was dropped off the needles. It generally will run down a row or two and then just sit there waiting to be noticed. To pick it back up, work across to the spot where the stitch has dropped. Lay the work out flat and, using a crochet hook the same diameter as the knitting needles, work the stitch back up to the needles.

Picking up a knit stitch

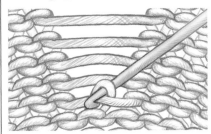

Picking up a purl stitch

1 Insert the hook into the dropped stitch and under the strand of yarn immediately above the loop on the hook. Catch the yarn in the hook.

2 Pull the strand through the loop on the hook.

3 Repeat until all strands have been hooked up and slip the last loop onto the left needle without twisting. Complete the row.

Extra Stitches

Extra stitches, or inadvertent increases, are a little different. If you have discovered them early or they aren't visible, you may be able to decrease at the edge of the work to counteract them. Knitting is very forgiving, and one or two extra stitches may not drastically change the shape of a piece. However, if extra stitches have added significant width to a piece or they are visible, the only recourse you have will be to pull the work back (also known as ripping back) and reknit. Checking for problems every so often so you won't have to rework as much is a good idea.

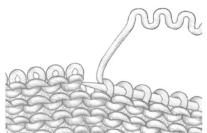

1 Slip the stitches off the needle and unravel down to one row above the mistake. Hold the work in your left hand and hold a smaller needle than used in the work in your right hand.

2 Insert the needle tip, from back to front and from right to left, into the stitch below the first loop. Pull gently on the yarn to unravel the loop. Continue along the row, picking up each stitch in turn along the row. Using the correct needle size, continue knitting in the pattern.

FINISHING

Careful finishing really does make a difference in how well your projects turn out, no matter how large or small. That one word—finishing—is really a set of skills and not just a few lines of instructions. The good news is that because it is a skill set, good finishing can be learned. The basic information here is a sound start, but there are more in-depth sources listed in the resources section. Like learning any new skill, be sure to practice new techniques and ask for help when in doubt.

TIP: The most useful, though not necessarily pleasant, tip for achieving good results with finishing is to just resign yourself to re-doing the finishing steps if the project doesn't come out right. Repeat until correct.

Blocking

Blocking is the process of smoothing and shaping the knitted pieces to the correct size and shape before assembling them. Depending on the yarn used, it can be the secret of success. Be sure to check the label; some novelty yarns, such as Lurex, should not be blocked or pressed.

There are two basic blocking methods: wet blocking and steam blocking. Wet blocking is the safer of the two and can be used on most fibers. To wet block a piece of knitting, lay it out on a large, flat, padded surface that will withstand moisture. Use rust-resistant pins to pin the pieces around the edges, gently shaping the item to the right size according to the pattern. Use a spray bottle to dampen the item, patting it gently to ensure the work is thoroughly damp. Leave the item pinned flat until completely dry.

To steam block, lay the knitting out as described above. Use a warm iron and a damp pressing cloth or a steam iron. Don't use the iron directly on the knitted surface and don't press the fabric. Pass the iron lightly over the damp press cloth or the surface of the work, letting the steam penetrate the item. Leave the piece pinned to shape and flat until it is cool and dry.

Seaming

Sewing up your finished project is a simple and straightforward process, but it can have a large effect on the final appearance. Knitting produces a soft, flexible fabric, and crooked or puckered seams can ruin all the effort you put into making the item.

To start, you will need a blunt-tipped needle, such as a bodkin or tapestry needle, with an eye large enough to accommodate the seaming yarn. Should you need to pin the pieces together, knitters pins are best as they are longer and have large heads to help prevent them from disappearing into the knitted fabric. You could use safety pins instead. Insert the pins at right angles to the edges.

Use the same yarn used to knit the pieces to sew them together. If you used a novelty yarn that would be hard to sew with, use a smooth, strong yarn in a matching or compatible color. Be sure that the seaming yarn can be cleaned in the same way as the rest of the project.

As you work, try to keep an even tension on the seam. Pull the yarn snug but not so tight that the edge or seam puckers. Try to leave a little "give" in the sewing yarn because this reduces the chance that it will break and will make a more comfortable seam.

An 18-in. (46cm) length of yarn is plenty for sewing. Pulling the yarn repeatedly through the fabric can cause it to break if it is too long.

Mattress Stitch

Here is a good all-purpose seaming stitch, often called "mattress stitch," to get you started. Be sure to keep your seams straight by always inserting your needle in the same

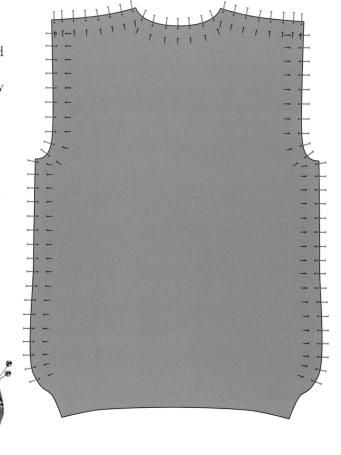

place along the seam. This seam is nearly invisible and does not make an unsightly or uncomfortable ridge.

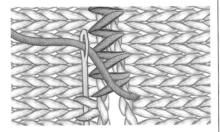

Stitching a side edge

Stitching a top edge

1 Working from the right side, insert the yarn needle under the bar between stitches. Then insert the needle under the corresponding bar on the other piece.

2 Continue along the seam for approximately 1 in. (2.5cm), then pull the yarn snug. Repeat until the seam is complete.

Backstitch

The backstitch seam is a strong and firm seam that is used where some structure and support would be desirable, such as the shoulder seam.

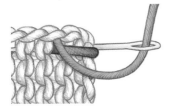

1 With right sides together and edges even, secure yarn at the edge. Insert the needle from front to back at the edge of the seam, and then bring it up from back to front a half stitch forward.

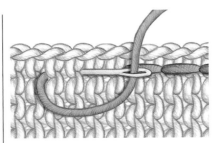

2 Insert the needle where the first stitch began and bring it up a whole stitch forward. * Insert the needle at the end of the previous stitch and up again a whole stitch forward. Repeat from the * working from right to left. With each stitch, you are going back a half stitch and forward a whole stitch. At the beginnings and ends of seams, weave the yarn tails back into the seam for 5 or 6 stitches and cut the yarn close to the work.

Buttons and Buttonholes

Buttonholes can be challenging. Because the fabric is so elastic, they can easily be too big to hold the button. If that happens, you can either use bigger buttons, which may spoil the look of the item, or you can sew the buttonhole up to make it smaller, which may leave a noticeable scar. It's best to make a swatch and test the button you want to use before beginning.

Sometimes you don't have to make buttonholes at all. Because the fabric is so elastic, you can use smaller buttons and carefully separate the stitches in the appropriate place and neatly stitch around the hole to keep it open. Presto! A nice, neat, and perfectly positioned buttonhole!

However, some patterns do benefit from using larger buttons that will require a proper buttonhole worked into the fabric. Work to where the buttonhole should be and make an opening.

Eyelet Buttonhole

This is simply a yarn over and a decrease. Work to the position desired, YO, k2tog, work to end of row.

Two-row Buttonhole

This buttonhole can be made any size and also works to form large openings in the work.

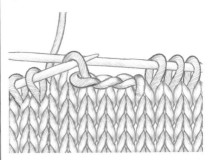

1 Work along the row to where you want the opening, BO number of stitches required, continue in pattern to the end of the row. There are four stitches shown bound off here, but remember—knitting is very stretchy so this will stretch to fit a much larger button than you think.

2 On the following row, work to the bound off stitches, cast on the same number of stitches as bound off, complete the row.

EMBELLISHMENT

In this book, embellishment is something that has been applied or added to the knitted project, rather than something worked into it like stripes. Embellishment is the perfect way to add a bit of your own personality to your work or, if the item is a gift, to make it truly special for the recipient by incorporating something special to him or her. These added details are what will make your projects truly unique and set them apart from something mass-produced and available in any store.

When choosing what to use to embellish your handwork, there are a few points to keep in mind. The weight of the addition must not be too heavy or it will cause the piece to stretch and sag. Check that the embellishment isn't likely to snag or pull the fabric. Most important, be sure the cleaning methods are compatible or that the trim is removable for cleaning if necessary.

You can find beads, buttons, cords, ribbons, beaded trims, and appliqués at fabric and craft stores. Make your own tassels, pom-poms, embroidery, knitted cord, and fringe for endless possibilities.

Tassels

This is one of my favorites—I just love tassels! Large and small, beaded and plain, tassels can be made from all types of fibers. Put them in unexpected places, such as collars and flaps.

Make tassels from all sorts of fibers.

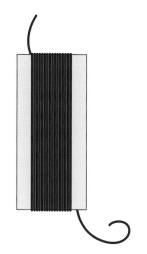

1 Cut a piece of cardboard 2 in. (5cm) wide and as long as you want the tassel. Wrap the yarn around the cardboard lengthwise. The more wraps, the larger your tassel will be.

2 Use a yarn needle to thread a length of yarn under the wrapped yarn, at the edge of the cardboard. Pull tightly and tie firmly. This is the top of your tassel.

3 Cut yarn at the bottom. Remove the cardboard.

4 Approximately ½ in. (1.3cm) from top of tassel, firmly tie another length of yarn around the "neck" of the tassel. Wrap yarn a few times, if you like. Trim bottom of tassel evenly.

Fringe

Fringe is a classic embellishment option, and it doesn't have to be at the end of a scarf. Try adding fringe to the bottom of a skirt or sleeve cuff.

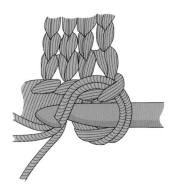

- Make simple fringe: Cut yarn twice the desired length with extra for knotting and fold the yarn in half over a crochet hook. From the wrong side of the work, insert the hook from front to back through the work. Pull the yarn ends through the work and loop; tighten. Finish all fringe before trimming to the desired length.

Pom-poms

Pom-poms are another classic add-on. Try using them in a new way by making small, elegant pom-poms out of luxurious fibers. They can be made the old-fashioned way with circles of cardboard, or you can try out some of the new pom-pom makers available now.

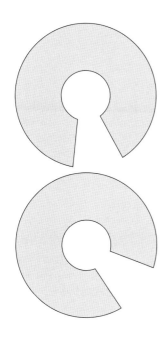

1 Cut two circles of cardboard the width of the pom-pom. Cut out the center hole and a pie-shaped wedge out of the circle.

Add some fun to your piece with pom-poms.

2 Hold the two circles together and wrap yarn tightly around the cardboard. Carefully cut the yarn at the outer edge of the cardboard. Leave the yarn as undisturbed as possible.

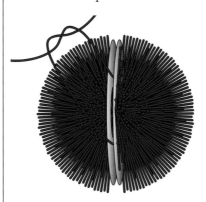

3 Tie a piece of yarn tightly between the two circles of yarn-wrapped cardboard. Remove the cardboard and trim.

Knitted Cord

Making knitted cord may seem mysterious or difficult because it involves double-pointed needles. Don't let that put you off! Once you have finished your first cord, you'll be looking for ways to use more of this fun and easy embellishment. Knitted cord can also be made with a knitting spool, or knitting knobby, as they used to be called. Once you learn to make it with knitting needles, though, you won't go back.

1 Cast on 3–5 stitches. Knit one row. Without turning the work, slide the stitches back to the other end of the needle.

2 Pull the yarn tightly from the bottom to the top and knit across.

3 Repeat steps 1 and 2 until your cord is the desired length. Cut yarn and thread end through stitches to secure.

FELTING

Felting is a rediscovered old technique that changes the basic shape and structure of knitted items. Technically, because it involves already-spun yarns made into fabric, it is "fulling." True felting starts with unspun wool fibers that are felted together to make a usable fabric. We will use felting, the more common term, in this book even though we really are fulling.

The process starts with yarns made of animal fibers that will felt and are free of special treatments to prevent felting. Many yarns on the market now will state on the label that they are suitable for felting. A finished project is usually started by knitting at a very loose gauge to produce an item that is substantially larger than the finished dimensions. Many people use washing machines to felt, using the hot water, agitation, and length of cycle it offers. Felting may be done by hand in the same manner, but it is significantly more work.

Why Wool Felts

Wool felts because microscopic scales encase the fibers. When the scales are smooth and lying flat, the fiber is equally smooth and tangle-free. Human hair also has scales

and acts the same way. When the scales are roughed up by chemical, thermal, or mechanical agents, they catch each other, and the fibers mat and shrink together. The agents that cause felting are soap (chemical), hot water and sudden temperature changes (thermal), and hand or machine agitation (mechanical). Once the fibers have matted together, the process is irreversible.

How to Felt

It's a good idea to put your knitted item in a zippered bag to collect the fuzz that it is going to release. This fuzz is a by-product of the felting process and in large amounts can damage your washing machine's water pump. Set the washing machine cycle for the lowest water level (smallest load) and heavy cycle (roughest agitation), and use the hottest water you can. Use a very small amount of laundry soap; start with only a tablespoon or two.

1 Start the washer and add your bagged project. You might want to add something to help roughen it up as the washer agitates—old jeans are a great choice. Towels leave little bits of fuzz that you will spend forever picking off later.

2 Let the washer agitate for about five minutes and check the process of the felting. You may find that the items haven't felted or may have gotten a bit larger. Not to worry—this is the early phase of the process when the scales are opening up and the heat and water are being absorbed into the fibers. Let the machine continue to work its magic, and keep checking every 5 or 10 minutes until your project is thoroughly felted.

3 Then, let the washer continue with the rinse and spin operations. If you are concerned that any further felting will be too much, do not let the machine agitate the item. Swish the project by hand in the tub, and then spin the water out.

Blocking Felted Items

Wet wool items, whether felted or not, are very pliable. The felted items can be shaped in any number of ways. Push and pull flat items into shape and dry flat. For shaped projects, seek out forms to use, such as head-sized bowls for hats and plastic bags to stuff purses. Leave the whole thing undisturbed until it is completely dry. Finish it up with a light brushing and a trim for stray fibers and fuzz.

A knit swatch before and after felting.

On a Personal Note

I am a haphazard felter. In spite of the careful instructions laid out above, I very often just throw things in the washing machine. The reason I know that towels lint and you will have to pick fuzz off is because I have done that in spite of good advice not to. Neither do I check my projects during the cycle; I just take my chances and see what comes out.

Absolutely do not approach your felting this way unless you are very comfortable with the idea of having to remake something entirely if it doesn't come out right. Remember that felting is irreversible. I know this too because I have had to remake a project a time or two.

Projects

Wearables

Simple Scarf

This scarf is an ideal first project. It's made with a simple garter stitch in a variegated yarn for interest. Practice your knitting while making yourself a unique accessory. Move on to the striped version for a different fashion option. Scarves make wonderful and personal gifts. The basic knit stitch is used to make the entire scarf, and there is no shaping and minimal finishing.

Finished Size: Approximately 6 x 48 in. (15cm x 1.2m), excluding trim	**Materials:** • **Yarns:** 100% acrylic variegated (84 yds./76m per skein) or 20% wool, 80% acrylic (108 yds./98m per skein), super-bulky weight yarn, 2 skeins per scarf • **Knitting needles:** size 15 (10mm), or size needed for gauge • **Tapestry or yarn needle** • **Tape measure** • **Scissors**		

Finished Size:
Approximately 6 x 48 in. (15cm x 1.2m), excluding trim

Techniques and Skills Used:
Cast on *(p. 19)*, **knit** *(p. 21)*, **bind off** *(p. 22)*, **weave in ends** *(p. 23)*

Finishing:
Fringe or tassels *(p. 28)*

Project Gauge:
8 stitches/4 in. (10cm) in garter stitch (knit every row)

Note: Gauge is not that important for a scarf since it doesn't need to fit precisely.

Materials:
• **Yarns:** 100% acrylic variegated (84 yds./76m per skein) or 20% wool, 80% acrylic (108 yds./98m per skein), super-bulky weight yarn, 2 skeins per scarf
• **Knitting needles:** size 15 (10mm), or size needed for gauge
• **Tapestry or yarn needle**
• **Tape measure**
• **Scissors**

Note: Use one skein of each color for the striped version.

Pattern Stitch for Gauge Swatch:
• CO 8 stitches.
• K every row for length.
Swatch measures 4 in. (10cm) wide.

SCARF
• CO 12 stitches.
• K every row until scarf measures 48 in. (1.2m) or length desired.
• BO and work ends in securely.

Striped Version
• Work 1–3 rows of color A, change to color B for another one to three rows. See "Joining New Yarn," *(p. 22)*. Try to vary the row counts as randomly as possible.
• BO and leave a 12 in. (30cm) tail and gather ends tightly. Weave in ends.

Finishing
• Attach fringe evenly along ends of scarf.

Striped Version
Make two chunky tassels about 5 in. (13cm) long and attach one to each gathered end.

TIP: Self-striping yarns are lovely and make their own color magic with very little effort.

YARN AND SUBSTITUTION INFORMATION

The yarns chosen for this project are super-bulky weight yarns. One is 100% acrylic in a bright variegated color, and the other is a solid-colored 20% wool, 80% acrylic blend. Yarn label information suggests 8 or 9 stitches to 4 in. (10cm) on size 13 (9mm) or 17 (12.75mm) needles. The strand is well twisted and rope-like with little surface sheen or fuzz.

To make your scarf with a different yarn, look for a yarn that will work to the approximate gauge. Be sure to make a swatch and double-check how much yarn you might need if you choose a significantly different type of yarn.

Almost any yarn will make an attractive scarf. While very textured or furry yarns may make a nice scarf, they can be more difficult to work with because the knobbly fibers will obscure the individual stitches. Make sure you like the look of the yarn and how it works before starting your scarf. Wool and wool blends are good choices for cold, wet climates. For milder winters, consider blends of other natural fibers, such as cotton and bamboo.

Creative Options

* Create a multicolored striped scarf by making each stripe a different color and width. Use all bright colors or all neutrals for a cohesive look.

* Use different textures of yarn (smooth, shiny, fuzzy, etc.) all in the same color for an understated striped effect. Black and off-white scarves are classic.

* Add a little sparkle with metallic yarn. Use it for a one-row stripe or as the finishing fringe or tassels.

* Try a classic heather tweed yarn for a man's scarf.

Snug Hoodie Scarf

What a great idea—a hood and scarf combined! This project will keep you toasty warm and stylish, too. Hoodie scarves are a great gift idea for just about anyone on your list; nearly everyone can use a scarf with a little something more. There are lots of ways to customize the finished project to make it your own.

Finished Size:	Materials:
Scarf: Approximately 42 x 10 in. (107 x 25cm) before finishing **Hood:** Approximately 10 x 10 in. (25 x 25cm)	• **Yarn:** 100% superwash wool worsted-weight yarn, 65 yds./59m per ball, 6 balls • **Knitting needles:** size 9 (5.5mm), or size needed for gauge • **Tapestry or yarn needle** • **Tape measure** • **Scissors**
Techniques and Skills Used: **Cast on** (p. 19), **knit** (p. 21), **purl** (p. 21), **pick up stitches** (p. 23), **bind off** (p. 22), **weave in ends** (p. 23)	*Note: The project as shown used all six balls of yarn completely. You may want to buy an extra ball to be sure you have enough material.*
Finishing: **Seaming** (p. 26), **attaching tassels** (p. 28)	**Pattern Stitch for Gauge Swatch:** The pattern stitch is called seed stitch. It is worked over an even number of stitches:
Project Gauge: 20 stitches/5½ in. (14cm) over pattern stitch *Note: Gauge is moderately important for this project. Check your gauge to see if you need to adjust the size of the needles.*	• CO 20 stitches. • **Row 1:** *K1, p1, repeat from *. • **Row 2:** *P1, k1, repeat from *. • Repeat rows 1 and 2 for length. Swatch measures 5½ in. (14cm) wide.

YARN AND SUBSTITUTION INFORMATION

The yarn chosen for this project is a worsted-weight 100% superwash wool yarn. Yarn label information suggests 4 stitches to 1 in. (2.5cm) with size 9 (5.5mm) needles. The plies are lightly and unevenly twisted, which enhances the slight sheen to give a softly textured look.

There are many other yarns that would make good substitutions, including many wool and natural fiber blends available, such as mohair, angora, and cashmere. For insulation from the cold, stick with these fibers, but in milder climates, consider organic cotton yarns or other natural fibers, such as linen or a cotton/linen blend in worsted weight.

You might want to try novelty and highly textured yarns for this project, but the texture will obscure the stitch pattern and may make working more difficult. Be sure to check the gauge first as well to make sure the finished item will be a reasonable size.

SCARF
• CO 36 stitches.
• **Row 1:** *K1, p1, repeat from *.
• **Row 2:** *P1, k1, repeat from *.
• Repeat rows 1 and 2 until piece measures 42 in. (1.07m) from beginning.
• BO in pattern and weave in ends.

Hood
• Fold scarf in half and mark the halfway point. Measure 10 in. (25cm) on either side and pm at those points.
• Pick up 72 stitches evenly between the outside markers.

TIP: Divide the distance between the markers into four sections. Pick up 18 stitches in each section by picking up approximately two stitches for every three rows, adjusting the stitch count to fit.

Begin Pattern on Picked-up Stitches
• **Row 1:** *K1, p1, repeat from *.
• **Row 2:** *P1, k1, repeat from *.
• Repeat rows 1 and 2 until hood measures 12 in. (30cm) from pick-up row.
• BO in pattern and weave in ends.

Finishing

- Fold in half and sew top of hood together.
- Make seven 3 in. (7.6cm) tassels of matching or contrasting yarn.
- Attach three tassels to each end, spacing them evenly along ends of scarf. Attach one tassel to point of the hood.

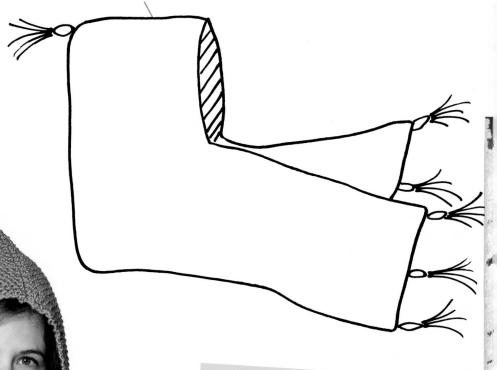

seam

Creative Options

✳ Color can make all the difference in the finished look of the project. Understated neutrals, like off-white, charcoal, and earth colors, lend a sophisticated air. Bold, dramatic colors, like red, hot pink, and other brights, sparkle with energy and fun.

✳ Try an evening hooded wrap with a soft and sparkly metallic yarn. For chilly nights, angora or cashmere is luxurious.

✳ Make the scarf longer—work to 72–84 in. (1.8–2.1m), and turn the ends up to make pockets.

✳ Use your imagination to trim the scarf. Explore the trimmings available, and experiment a bit. Just make sure that cleaning requirements for the yarn and the trimmings are similar.

Classic Hat

This is the basic knit hat that everyone wears and wants. Hats are great gifts for all your friends—even the guys! They are useful and stylish, and you only need one ball of most yarns. Make a whole wardrobe of hats!

Finished Size:
To fit average adult, approximately 21 in. (53cm) circumference

Techniques and Skills Used:
Cast-on *(p. 19)*, **knit** *(p. 21)*, **purl** *(p. 21)*, **increase** *(p. 22)*, **bind off** *(p. 22)*, **weave in ends** *(p. 23)*

Finishing:
Seaming *(p. 26)*, **attaching tassels** *(p. 28)*

Project Gauge:
18 stitches/5¼ in. (13cm) in stockinette stitch

Materials:
- **Yarn:** 53% wool, 47% acrylic bulky-weight yarn, 100 yds./92 m per ball, 1 ball
- **Knitting needles:** size 9 (5.5mm) or size needed for gauge
- **Tapestry or yarn needle**
- **Tape measure**
- **Scissors**

Pattern Stitch for Gauge Swatch:
The pattern stitch is plain stockinette stitch.
- CO 18 stitches.
- **Row 1 and all right-side (odd) rows**: K.
- **Row 4**: K2, p14, k2.
- Repeat for length.
Swatch measures 5¼ in. (13cm) wide.

YARN AND SUBSTITUTION INFORMATION

The yarn chosen for this project is a heavy, but lofty and soft, wool and acrylic blend. Yarn label information suggests a knit gauge of 13 stitches to 4 in. (4cm) on size 11 (8mm) needles. It is a very lightly spun yarn with thick-and-thin portions. The surface is not fuzzy.

You can achieve the same effect by choosing a bulky-weight yarn with little twist and lots of loft in either 100% wool, a blend, or even 100% acrylic, as long as the yarn is soft and fluffy. Highly textured yarns, such as fur or eyelash yarns, could produce a nice effect, but they may be difficult to work with. Be sure to make a swatch and check the gauge.

This is a great project for trying out different yarns and fibers—almost anything might make a nice hat!

HAT
- CO 8 stitches.
- **Row 1:** K.
- **Row 2 and all wrong-side rows:** P.
- **Row 3:** Increase in each stitch across (16 stitches).
- **Row 5:** *Increase in first stitch, k1, repeat from * across (24 stitches).
- **Row 7:** *Increase in first stitch, k2, repeat from * across (32 stitches).
- **Row 9:** *Increase in first stitch, k3, repeat from * across (40 stitches).
- **Row 11:** *Increase in first stitch, k4, repeat from * across (48 stitches).
- **Row 13:** *Increase in first stitch, k5, repeat from * across (56 stitches).
- **Row 15:** *Increase in first stitch, k6, repeat from * across (64 stitches).
- **Row 17:** *Increase in first stitch, k7, repeat from * across (72 stitches).
- **Row 19:** K.
- **Row 20:** P.

Begin Ribbing
- **Row 21:** K2, p2 across row.
- Continue in k2, p2 rib until ribbing measures 3 in. (7.6cm) or desired length.
- BO in rib, leaving a 12-in. (30cm) length of yarn for seaming.

TIP: When binding off a piece worked in a pattern, keep the bind-off row in the pattern as well by working each stitch on the left-hand needle according to the stitch pattern. This is binding off in pattern.

Finishing
- Sew back seam using mattress stitch *(p. 26)*.
- Stitch around opening at top and tighten to close.
- Work all ends in.
- Make a large tassel about 6 in. (15cm) long. Attach to top center of hat, adding a large bead if desired.

Creative Options

* After shaping, make the hat as long as you want. Then work the ribbing and complete as instructed.

* Omit the ribbing for a soft, curled edge and make the body longer to allow for the curl. Stockinette curls to the right side, so most stockinette pieces are edged with ribbing or garter stitch to keep the finished piece flat.

Glam Gauntlets

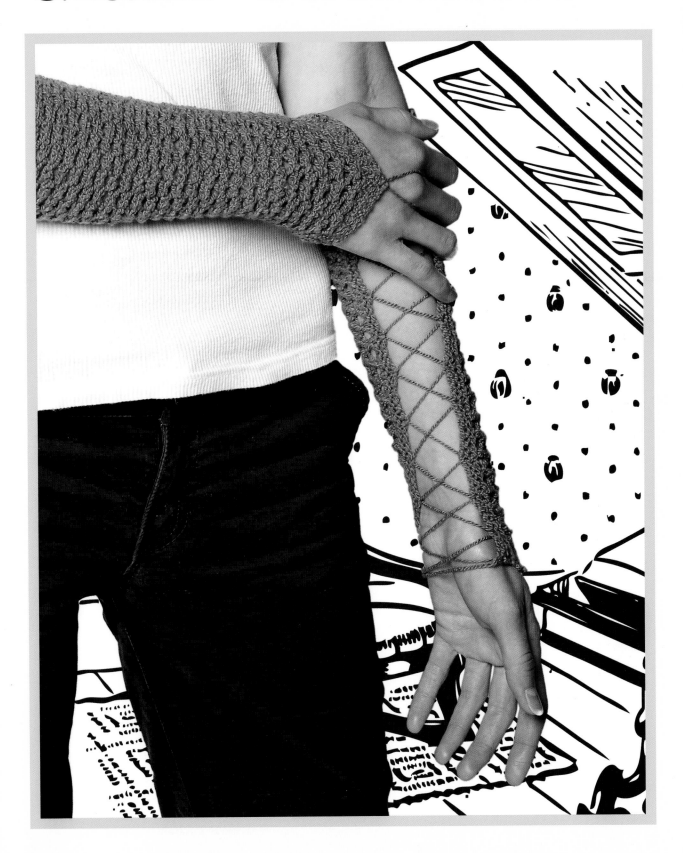

Elastic yarn and an open pattern make a fun mesh fabric. These gauntlets are perfect for when you're feeling adventurous and want all eyes on you. This project is an example of "negative ease." The finished item is smaller than the body part it fits. That is why using stretch fiber is so important. Good-quality wool with lots of natural resilience may work for this project, but the snug fit will be altered. These gauntlets will stretch above the elbow. See "Creative Options" for a shorter length.

YARN AND SUBSTITUTION INFORMATION

The yarn chosen for this project is a light worsted-weight 98.3% cotton and 1.7% elastic yarn. Yarn label information suggests 29 stitches to 4 in. (10cm) on size 4 or 5 (3.5 or 3.75mm) needles. The yarn strand is slightly textured and puckered due to the elastic content and has a matte, slightly fuzzy surface.

Due to the snug fit of this project, substituting other yarns requires careful thought. Any yarn with some stretch, such as elastic or Lycra, should work. If you choose a yarn without stretch fibers, please be sure to make a generous swatch and test the fit before proceeding. This yarn is able to stretch about 66% from its original length.

GAUNTLETS

TIP: There are four edge stitches instead of the two used in the swatch.

- CO 65 stitches.
- **Rows 1–3:** K.
- **Row 4:** K4, p57, k4.
- **Row 5:** K4, *YON2, k2tog, repeat from * to last four stitches, k4.
- **Row 6:** K4, p across to last two stitches dropping extra wrap, k4.
- **Row 7:** K4, *k2tog, YON2, repeat from * to last four stitches, k4.
- **Row 8:** K4, p across to last two stitches dropping extra wrap, k4.
- Repeat rows 5–8 until piece measures approximately 3¾ in. (9.5cm) from beginning edge, ending with row 8.
- Next three rows: K.
- BO and weave in ends.
- Make two.

Finished Size:
Approximately 11 in. (28cm) long, unstretched

Techniques and Skills Used:
Cast on (p. 19), **knit** (p. 21), **purl** (p. 21), **yarn over** (p. 22), **weave in ends** (p. 23)

Finishing:
Lacing, attaching yarn loop

Project Gauge:
20 stitches/3½ in. (8.8cm) over pattern stitch

Note: The gauge is not too important for this project. The elasticity of the yarn is very forgiving. Just make sure your swatch is not too small.

Materials:
- **Yarn:** 98.3% cotton, 1.7% elastic light worsted-weight yarn, 100 yds./91m per ball, 1 ball
- **Knitting needles:** size 5 (3.75mm) or size needed for gauge
- **Tapestry or yarn needles**
- **Tape measure**

Pattern Stitch for Gauge Swatch:
The pattern stitch is worked over a multiple of 3 stitches.

- CO 20 stitches.
- **Rows 1–3:** K.
- **Row 4:** P.
- **Row 5:** K2, *YON2, k2tog, repeat from * to last two stitches, k2.
- **Row 6:** K2, p across to last two stitches dropping extra wrap, k2.
- **Row 7:** K2, *k2tog, YON2, repeat from * to last two stitches, k2.
- **Row 8:** K2, p across to last two stitches dropping extra wrap, k2.
- Repeat rows 5–8 for length.
Swatch measures 3½ in. (8.8cm) wide.

Note: YON2 means to wrap the yarn around the needle twice.

Finishing

- Cut a 60-in. (1.5 m) length of yarn, and thread both ends into yarn needles.
- Loosely and evenly lace up long sides of gauntlet at approximately 1-in. (2.5cm) intervals.
- Try on gauntlet, adjust lacing, and tie to secure.
- Cut a 12-in. (30cm) length of yarn, thread yarn needle, and secure to bottom edge of gauntlets.
- At center bottom, secure yarn and make a 1-in. (2.5cm) loop as middle finger catcher.
- Weave end in.

TIP: If you use a yarn with less elasticity, you might want to use elastic cord as a lacing to add some stretch.

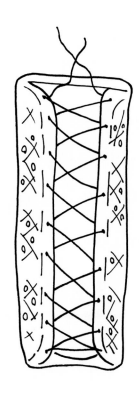

Creative Options

* Color choice makes a big difference in the finished look. Black is glam and dramatic; bright colors are fun and fashionable. Make a pair of gauntlets to match your favorite party dress!

* Wear your favorite bracelet or cuff over the gauntlet for a distinctive look.

* Make a half-length pair by casting on 35 stitches. Complete as directed.

How to Handle Loops

What to do with that extra wrap on the needle? As you purl the wrapped stitch, purl through only one loop of the wraps. Then simply drop the extra wrap off the needle when slipping the newly purled stitch from the left to the right needle.

The YON2 makes a much larger hole than a standard yarn-over. Because the yarn is so stretchy, a single-loop yarn-over just disappears into the fabric. The extra loop adds some drama to the stitch pattern.

Cozy Headbands

Stay toasty warm—and stylish, too. These two headbands, one with a stockinette welt pattern and one with a flat rib, are great for holding your hair back and keeping your ears warm. Make several for yourself and for friends. They work up quickly and use only small amounts of yarn. These headbands offer the perfect opportunity to try some wonderful cashmere or angora that you've been eyeing.

YARN AND SUBSTITUTION INFORMATION

The yarn chosen for this project is a substantial worsted-weight 100% wool yarn. Yarn label information suggests 20 stitches to 4 in. (10cm) on size 7 (4.5mm) needles. This yarn looks and feels exactly like worsted-weight yarn should; it is a nicely twisted strand with a matte surface that isn't hairy or fuzzy.

Many yarns would make good substitutions for this project. Wool and natural-fiber blends, such as mohair, angora, cashmere, and similar fibers, would be good choices. For milder climates, consider an organic cotton yarn or other natural fibers, such as linen or a cotton/linen blend in worsted weight.

You might want to conside novelty and highly textured yarns for this project, as they would make an attractive headband. Be aware that the texture will obscure the stitch patterns, which will make working more difficult. Also be sure to check the gauge first to make sure the band will fit.

STOCKINETTE WELT GATHERED HEADBAND

- CO 28 stitches.
- K2 rows, begin pattern rows, keeping two stitches at each edge in garter stitch.

TIP: Instructions to "keep stitches at each edge in garter stitch" are often used in knitting directions. It means to knit the first two stitches of every row and then follow the detailed instructions for that row. Place stitch markers to separate the two edge stitches.

Finished Size:
To fit an average adult, approximately 19 in. (48cm) long, stretches to 20–21 in. (51–53cm)

Techniques and Skills Used:
Cast on (p. 19), **knit** (p. 21), **purl** (p. 21), **bind off** (p. 22), **weave in ends** (p. 23)

Finishing:
Seaming (p. 26), **gathering**

Project Gauge:
Stockinette welt, 20 stitches/5 in. (13cm) over pattern stitch
Flat rib, 20 stitches/ 4½ in. (11cm), slightly stretched

Note: Gauge is moderately important for this project. The bands are worked lengthwise so you can adjust the fit as you work; the gauge will affect the finished width.

Materials:
- **Yarn:** 100% wool worsted-weight yarn, 223 yds./204m per skein, 1 skein
- **Knitting needles:** size 8 (5mm) or size needed for gauge
- **Tapestry or yarn needle**
- **Tape measure**
- **Scissors**

Pattern Stitch for Gauge Swatch: Stockinette Welt:
- CO 20 stitches.
- **Rows 1, 3, 5**: K.
- **Rows 2, 4**: P.
- **Row 6**: K.
- **Row 7**: P.
- **Row 8**: K.
- Repeat rows 1–8 for length. Swatch measures 5 in. (13cm) wide.

TIP: The pattern stitch is five rows of stockinette stitch alternated with three rows of reverse stockinette stitch to form welts.

Flat Rib:
Note: This stitch is a flat ribbing worked over a multiple of 5 stitches.
- CO 20 stitches.
- **Row 1**: K3, p2 across.
- **Row 2**: K2, p3 across.
- Repeat rows 1 and 2 for length. Swatch measures 4½ in. (11cm) wide when slightly stretched.

- **Rows 1, 3, 5:** K.
- **Rows 2, 4:** P.
- **Row 6:** K.
- **Row 7:** P.
- **Row 8:** K.
- Repeat rows 1–8 until piece measures 19 in. (48cm) long.
- K2 rows, BO.
- Weave in ends securely.

Gathered Headband

- Cut eight 16 in. (41cm) lengths of yarn. Thread yarn needle and secure end at edge of band. Weave yarn length in and out of center of reverse stockinette welt. Gather to approximately 3 in. (7.6cm). Secure yarn and weave in ends. Repeat on every other welt.

Flat Rib Headband

- CO 20 stitches.
- **Row 1:** K3, p2 across.
- **Row 2:** K2, p3 across.
- Repeat rows 1 and 2 until piece measures 4 in. (10cm) from beginning, ending with row 2.
- Increase row (RS): Increase in the first and last stitch of the k3 ribs (28 stitches on needle). You now have k5, p2 ribbing.
- Continue in wider ribbing until piece measures 15 in. (38cm) from beginning, ending with row 2.
- Decrease row (RS): Decrease at beginning and end of each k5 rib (20 stitches on needle). Return to k3, p2 ribbing.
- Continue until piece measures 19 in. (48cm).
- BO and weave in ends.

Finishing

- Sew ends together.

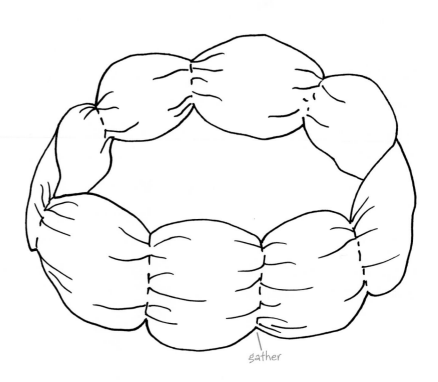

gather

Creative Options

* Color can make all the difference. Vary the colors to suit your winter wardrobe and personality. A soft cream wool will be an understated natural look, and a vivid color is fun and youthful.

* Go comfy with angora or formal with a metallic yarn. Just make sure that it's not scratchy on your skin.

* Try a variegated camouflage in the flat-rib version for a boy.

* Work either version in stripes of all kinds.

Fancy Fingerless Gloves

A dressier version of an old standby with ribbing for a snug fit, these gloves are perfect for cold offices and workplaces or even a breezy fall day at an outdoor café. Vary the length to suit your preference and wardrobe, or make a pair as a gift for a warmhearted friend. The longer version looks great with short sleeves.

Finished Size:
6½ (7½) in./17 (19) cm in circumference; larger size listed second in parenthesis

Techniques and Skills Used:
Cable cast on *(p. 20)*, **knit** *(p. 21)*, **purl** *(p. 21)*, **increase (optional)** *(p. 22)*, **bind off** *(p. 22)*, **weave in ends** *(p. 23)*

Finishing:
Seaming *(p. 26)*, **elastic casing**

Project Gauge:
20 stitches/3 in. (7.6cm) unstretched over k1, p1 rib

Materials:
- **Yarn:** 100% bamboo worsted-weight yarn, 77 yds./70m per skein, 2 skeins
- **Knitting needles:** size 6 (4mm) or size needed for gauge
- **Clear elastic:** ⅜-in. (1cm) wide, 20 in. (51cm), cut into two 10-in. (25.5cm) lengths
- **Tapestry or yarn needle**
- **Tape measure**
- **Scissors**

Note: Natural fibers are generally the most comfortable to wear in both cold and warm weather. Use bamboo, silk, or cotton for warm climates, and choose wool or cashmere for cold climates.

Pattern Stitch for Gauge Swatch:
The pattern stitch is k1, p1 ribbing worked over an even number of stitches.
- CO 20 stitches.
- **Row 1**: K1, p1, repeat to end of row.
- Repeat row 1.
Swatch measures 3 in. (7.6cm) wide

- Knit the next WS row.
- BO in knit.
- Work ends in securely.
- Make two.

Finishing
- With right sides together, sew opening closed 1¾ in. (4.4cm) from finger opening. Leave thumb opening for 1¾ in. (4.4cm), and sew remaining seam.

Elastic Casing
- Cut a 36-in. (91cm) length of yarn. Using yarn needle and attaching securely at side seam, sew a series of Xs loosely around inside of top of ribbing. Secure other end at side seam.
- Thread elastic through casing. Try glove on, tighten elastic to fit, and knot ends.

YARN AND SUBSTITUTION INFORMATION

The yarn used in these gloves is a worsted-weight 100% bamboo yarn. Bamboo is one of the new renewable fiber sources. Yarn label information suggests 5 stitches to 1 in. (2.5cm) with a size 7 (4.5mm) needle. The yarn is very lightly twisted and has a soft sheen with no fuzziness. The yarn resembles silk.

Other good choices would be a silk or silk blend, cashmere, mohair, or fine merino wool. To keep the dressy look of the original, choose smooth yarns with a soft sheen.

Avoid highly textured yarns unless you want a more casual and bulky look. Work a swatch to make sure the finished look is appealing.

GLOVES
- Use cable CO.
- CO 44 (48) stitches.
- Begin k1, p1 ribbing.
- Work until piece measures approximately 7 in. (18cm) for long length or 5 in. (13cm) for short gloves.
- Bind off in pattern if not working optional ruffle.

Ruffle
- Increase row: Increase one stitch in each stitch across (88, 96 st).
- Purl across (this becomes the wrong side).
- Knit across (right side).
- Continue in stockinette stitch until ruffle measures approximately 1½ in. (3.8cm), ending with a RS row.

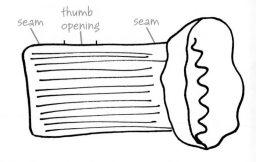

seam   thumb opening   seam

Creative Options

※ Make several shorter pairs to coordinate with your wardrobe.

※ Choose a special yarn to make a ruffled pair for dressing up.

※ Sew sparkling seed beads or sequin trim along the edge of the ruffle.

※ Use self-striping yarns for a fun, casual look.

Felted Tote

Make and felt an elegant accessory for your wardrobe. Felting makes this small tote bag thick and sturdy, so things you put inside will stay inside. It's perfect for holding your smaller knitting projects when you're out and about.

Pre-felting Dimensions:
13 in. (33cm) wide x
15 in. (38cm) tall x 3 in.
(7.6cm) deep

Finished Size:
10 in. (25cm) wide x
8 in. (20cm) tall x 3 in.
(7.6cm) deep after felting

Techniques and Skills Used:
Cast on *(p. 19)*, **knit** *(p. 21)*, **purl** *(p. 21)*, **pick up stitches** *(p. 23)*, **circular knitting** *(p. 24)*, **bind off** *(p. 22)*, **weave in ends** *(p. 23)*

Finishing:
Felting *(p. 30)*, **assembly**, **attaching tassels** *(p. 28)*, **backstitching** *(p. 27)*

Project Gauge:
Before felting:
20 stitches/5½ in. (14cm) in stockinette stitch
After felting:
20 stitches/4½ in. (11cm) in stockinette stitch

Note: Gauge is not critical for this project, and it won't be exact due to the felting process. Just be sure the after-felting measurements are close to the listed dimensions—larger is better than smaller.

Materials:
- **Yarn:** 100% pure merino wool worsted-weight yarn, 216 yds./197m per skein, kettle-dyed variegated colors, 2 skeins
- **Knitting needles:** size 10.5 (6.5mm), 24 in. (61cm) long, or size needed for gauge
- **4 decorative buttons:** ¾–1 in. (1.9–2.5cm)
- **Decorative chain:** 12 in. (30cm)
- **Strong thread or cord in coordinating color for assembly**
- **Skein of embroidery floss for decorative tassel**
- **Crewel or large sewing needle**
- **Tape measure**
- **Scissors**

Pattern Stitch for Gauge Swatch:
The pattern stitch is plain stockinette stitch.
- CO 20 stitches.
- **Rows 1–3**: K.
- **Row 4**: K2, p15, k2.
- **Row 5 and all succeeding right-side (odd) rows**: K.
- Repeat rows 4 and 5 for length.
- Knit last three rows and BO.
Swatch measures 5½ in. (14cm) wide before felting. After felting swatch as for project, it measures about 4½ in. (11cm) wide.

YARN AND SUBSTITUTION INFORMATION

This handy bag is made of a 100% merino wool. The yarn is worsted weight and soft, with little twist to the strand. Yarn label information suggests 4–5 stitches per 1 in. (2.5cm), with a needle sizes ranging from size 7–9 (4.5–5.5mm). The low twist gives the strand a soft, slightly fuzzy surface with no shine.

The only type of yarn that will produce a suitable finish is wool or a wool blend that has not been treated to be washable. Other yarns will not felt properly, so be sure to select one that will felt. Avoid yarns labeled "superwash."

This project was worked in a strongly variegated hand-dyed yarn. While the variegation adds great interest to this project, a solid color would be attractive.

TOTE BASE
- CO 46 stitches.
- Work in stockinette stitch until piece measures 4½ in. (11cm). Do not end yarn.

Pick Up and Work Sides
- Pick up 16 stitches along first short edge, 46 stitches on second long edge, and 16 stitches on last short edge (124 stitches).
- Knit around picked-up stitches to begin sides. Continue to work in the round, knitting every round, until sides measure 16 in. (41cm) from beginning.
- BO and weave in ends.

Make Straps

- CO 8 stitches, work in stockinette stitch to 32 in. (81cm).
- BO and weave in ends.
- Make two.

Felt

- Felt *(p. 30)*.

TIP: Don't worry about the shape of the straps—they will curl as they felt to form rounded handles.

Assembly

- Using a sharp needle and the strong thread or cord, sew handles to the outside of the bag. Make sure the handles are spaced evenly. Backstitch a square on each strap end through both thicknesses for security.
- Repeat for second strap.
- Attach ends of decorative chain to each strap end, and sew decorative button over ends.
- Make tassel from embroidery floss, and attach to one button.

backstitch a square on each strap end.

Creative Options

* Instead of variegated yarn, use multiple colors and work in random stripes. Try to keep the yarn weights similar so the finished item will felt evenly.

* Make broad stripes (2–4 in./5–10cm) in each of two or three related colors, then choose one of the colors to band the top and make the straps.

* Attach fringe or bead trim around the top of the bag and experiment with different materials for the straps. Try rope, chain, or cording.

Felted Waist Cincher

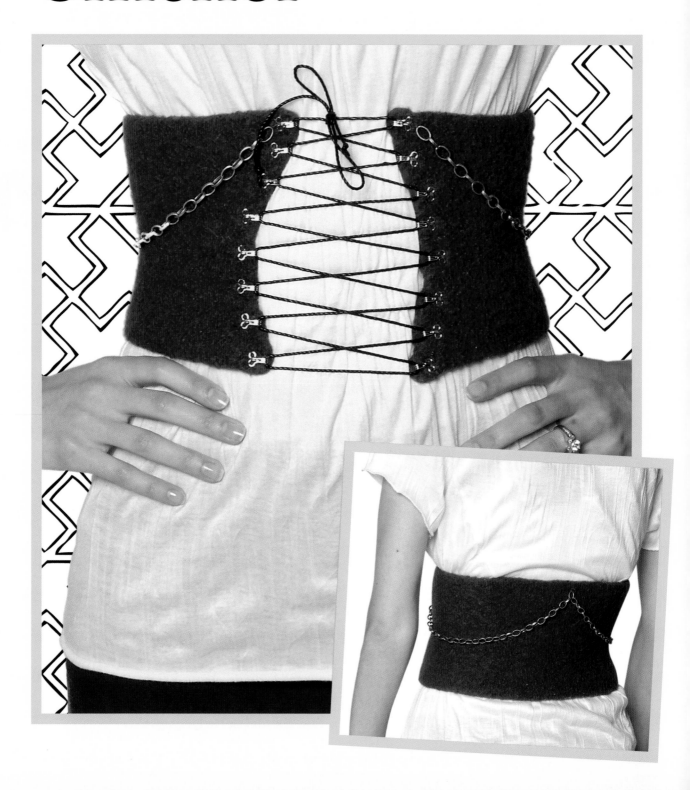

This is definitely an eye-catching, fashion-forward accessory. It is felted for structure and cinching ability. Add your own special touches for a feminine or more daring look. For the best fit, select finished waist size and add 3–6 in. (7.6–15cm) for the front opening.

Finished Size:
19 (20, 24, 28) in./48 (51, 61, 71) cm at waist; finished sizes may vary

Materials:
- **Yarn:** 100% wool worsted-weight yarn, 223 yds./204m per skein, 1 (1, 2, 2) skeins
- **Knitting needles:** size 10 (6mm) or size needed for gauge
- **Strong cotton cording:** for lacing, 36 in. (91cm)
- **Decorative chain:** approximately 25 in. (63cm)
- **Dressmaker hooks:** 16 size 3 (from hook-and-eye sets)
- **Sewing thread to match yarn**
- **Sewing needle**
- **Tapestry or yarn needle**
- **Tape measure**
- **Scissors**

Techniques and Skills Used:
Cast on *(p. 19)*, **knit** *(p. 21)*, **purl** *(p. 21)*, **weave in ends** *(p. 23)*, **decrease** *(p. 22)*, **increase** *(p. 22)*, **bind off** *(p. 22)*

Finishing:
Felting *(p. 30)*, **attaching hardware and trims**

Project Gauge:
Before felting:
20 stitches/5¼ in. (13cm) over stockinette stitch
After felting:
20 stitches/4½ in. (11cm)

Note: Gauge is not that important for this project, and it won't be exact after felting.

Pattern Stitch for Gauge Swatch:
The pattern stitch is plain stockinette.
- CO 20 stitches.
- **Row 1 and all RS (odd) rows**: K.
- **Rows 2 and 3**: K.
- **Row 4**: K2, p16, k2.
- Repeat rows 3 and 4 for length. Swatch measures 5¼ in. (13cm) wide before felting. Swatch measures approximately 4½ in. (11cm) wide after felting.

Mark Your Sizes

It is common in knitting instructions to see the directions written for the smallest size with larger sizes sequentially in parentheses. To be sure you catch all the notes pertaining to your size and don't accidentally work the wrong set of instructions, read all the way through the instructions before starting, and mark your size with a highlighter or pen. If you don't want to mark the original pattern, make a copy for your personal use.

YARN AND SUBSTITUTION INFORMATION

The yarn chosen for this project is a substantial worsted-weight 100% wool yarn. Yarn label information suggests 20 stitches to 4 in. (10cm) on size 7 (4.5mm) needles. This yarn looks and feels exactly like worsted wool should; it is a nicely twisted strand with a matte surface that is not hairy or fuzzy.

When choosing yarn for this project, please note that the only type of yarn that will produce a suitable finish is wool or a wool blend that has not been treated to be washable. Other yarns will not felt properly, so choose wool and avoid yarns labeled "superwash."

CINCHER

TIP: Directions are for size small; larger sizes are in parentheses. Consider how tightly you want to lace your cincher. If you like it looser, choose a larger size.

- CO 105 (111, 129, 150) stitches.
- **Row 1:** K.
- **Row 2 and all WS rows:** P.
- **Row 3:** K.
- **Row 5:** K3, dec 1, k31 (34, 39, 46), dec 1, k29 (29, 37, 44), dec 1, k31 (34, 39, 46), dec 1, k3 (101, 107, 125, 146) stitches.
- **Row 7:** K.
- **Row 9:** K.
- **Row 11:** K3, dec 1, k30 (33, 38, 45), dec 1, k27 (27, 35, 42), dec 1, k30 (33, 38, 45), dec 1, k93 (97, 103, 121, 142) stitches.
- Continue on 97 (103, 121, 142) stitches until 32 rows or 5 in. (13cm) have been worked, ending with purl row.

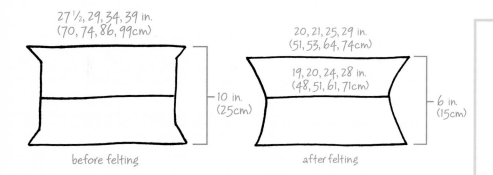

27 ½, 29, 34, 39 in.
(70, 74, 86, 99cm)

10 in.
(25cm)

before felting

20, 21, 25, 29 in.
(51, 53, 64, 74cm)

19, 20, 24, 28 in.
(48, 51, 61, 71cm)

6 in.
(15cm)

after felting

- Next RS row: Sl 1, k1 across.

TIP: To slip a stitch, insert the right needles as if to purl, and move the stitch over without working it.

- Next WS row: P1, sl 1 across.
- Resume stockinette stitch and begin second half:
- **Row 1:** K.
- **Row 2 and all WS rows:** P.
- **Rows 3–20:** Continue in stockinette stitch.
- **Row 21:** K3, inc 1, k30 (33, 38, 45), inc 1, k27 (27, 35, 42), inc 1, k30 (33, 38, 45), inc 1, k3 (101, 107, 125, 146 stitches).
- **Row 23:** K.
- **Row 25:** K.
- **Row 27:** K3, inc 1, k31 (34, 39, 46), inc 1, k29 (29, 37, 44), inc 1, k31 (34, 39, 46), inc 1, k3 (105, 111, 129, 150 stitches).
- **Rows 28–32:** Continue in stockinette stitch on 105 (111, 129, 150) stitches. Second half will measure approximately 5 in. (13cm) from center.
- BO and weave in ends.

TIP: Be sure the two halves measure the same distance from the center.

Felt
- Felt *(p. 30).*

Finishing
- Using matching sewing thread and needle, attach 8 hooks to

each front edge, spacing them evenly along the edge.
- Sew cording at halfway point to cincher at bottom eye. This will make it easier to put on and lace, as well as keep the cording even.

TIP: The hooks will bear most of the strain of lacing the cincher, so be certain they are attached securely. Don't trim the cord until after you have laced the cincher. It takes a surprising amount of cord to lace!

Pick Lifted Increases

The increase stitches won't show in the finished item. Just don't use a yarn-over increase, or you'll have a hole in the fabric. Use a make-one increase instead.

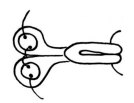

Creative Options

* Choose a color that suits your wardrobe and style. Go for pure drama with black yarn, hardware, and trim, or try using off-white yarn with faded silk roses for a soft, romantic look.

* Try different lacing options, like silken cord or ribbon. Just be sure the the lacing is strong enough to be pulled tight and sturdy enough to withstand being wound through the hooks.

* For a fun look, try using buttons instead of hooks or experiment with other hardware choices, such as grommets. Try out the method on a sample first, and remember that the edge has to be strong enough to pull the laces tight.

Flirty Skirt

This fun and flirty skirt is perfect for warm weather. The feminine flounce at the hem adds interest but doesn't overwhelm your figure. This project is worked in the round for easy knitting, and it is ideal for trying out circular knitting because it is very simple with minimal shaping.

When choosing a yarn for a garment like a skirt, avoid any of the characteristics that add bulk to the finished item. These include thick, stiff, hairy, fuzzy, and very shiny yarns. Be careful to choose a yarn that is not too heavy—pick a soft yarn that will make a drapable fabric. Work a swatch to test any yarn you are not sure about.

TIP: The smooth surface and soft drape of stockinette fabric is very flattering for knitted skirts.

Finished Size:
Approximately 37 (41, 44, 48) in. (94cm, 1.0, 1.1, 1.2m) at hip

Note: The waistband sits approximately 1 in. (2.5 cm) below the natural waist. Finished sizes include ease.

Techniques and Skills Used:
Cast on (p. 19), **knit** (p. 21), **purl** (p. 21), **circular knitting** (p. 24), **increase** (p. 22), **bind off** (p. 22), **weave in ends** (p. 23)

Finishing:
Seaming (p. 26), **inserting elastic**

Project Gauge:
20 stitches/4½ in. (11cm) over stockinette stitch

Note: Gauge is very important for this project. Check your gauge carefully and adjust as needed.

Materials:
- **Yarn:** 75% cotton, 25% acrylic light worsted-weight yarn, 110 yds./101m per ball, 6 (6, 7, 8) balls
- **Knitting needles:** 24 in. (61cm) circular needles size 6 (4mm) or size needed for gauge and one size smaller for waistband
- **Elastic:** ¾ in. (1.9cm) wide, approximately 45 in. (1.1m) long
- **Sewing thread and needle to secure elastic**
- **Tapestry or yarn needle**
- **Tape measure**
- **Scissors**
- **Stitch markers**

Pattern Stitch for Gauge Swatch:
The pattern stitch is plain stockinette stitch.
- CO 20 stitches.
- **Rows 1–3**: K.
- **Row 4**: K2, p to last two stitches, k2.
- **Row 5**: K.
- Repeat rows 4 and 5 for length.
- Knit last three rows.
- BO.
Swatch measures 4½ in. (11cm) wide.

SKIRT
Note: Directions are written for small size; larger sizes are in parentheses.

Waistband
- With smaller needle, CO 124 (134, 146, 160) stitches loosely.
- Join to begin working in round, and mark beginning and halfway points with stitch markers on round. Knit every row for 1–2 in. (2.5–5cm).
- Purl one row, and switch to larger needles.

TIP: Use the larger needle to cast on, and then transfer the stitches to the smaller needle before joining to make sure the cast-on edge is not too tight. The purl row gives a nice edge to the folded casing.

Body of Skirt
- Knit one round plain and begin increases at markers at beginning of round and halfway. (See "Increases" on following page.)
- Increase round: *Increase one stitch, knit two stitches, increase one stitch, work to second marker and repeat from *.
- Work two rounds plain.
- Alternate these two rounds until 176 (200, 214, 232) stitches are on needle.

YARN AND SUBSTITUTION INFORMATION
The yarn chosen for this project is light worsted-weight 75% cotton, 25% acrylic bouclé yarn. Yarn label information suggests 5.5 stitches to 1 in. (2.5cm) with size 6 (4mm) needles. It is a moderately textured yarn with a cabled twist and a matte slightly fuzzy surface. Other good choices would be an organic cotton yarn or other natural fiber, such as linen or a cotton/linen blend in light worsted weight.

- Work even to 19 (20, 21, 21) in./ 48 (51, 53, 53) cm from beginning of work or desired length (minus flounce).

Flounce

- Increase in each stitch around 352 (400, 428, 464) stitches.
- Work even until flounce measures 1½ in. (3.8cm).
- BO and weave in ends.

Finishing

- Fold band to inside and sew lightly to inside of skirt, using yarn needle threaded with yarn. Leave an opening to insert elastic.
- Thread elastic through casing, around band, and out through same opening. Adjust length, and secure with sewing thread and needle. Trim any excess elastic.

Increases

Place a second marker after the two knit stitches to help you keep these stitches in plain knitting for the increase rounds. This keeps the shaping from causing a bias twist in the skirt.

Which increase should you use? In this case, choose the most invisible, a make-one increase. Make one by lifting a new stitch from the stitch below.

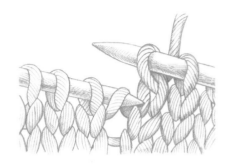

Make-one increase

Stitch Charts

The chart shown is another way of presenting the information in the row-by-row instructions. While a chart may look intimidating at first, it really has a system and an order. Many knitters find charts easier to use. See "Charts" *(p. 12)*, for information about reading the chart.

| | knit on right side rows, purl on wrong side rows |
| V | increase from row below |

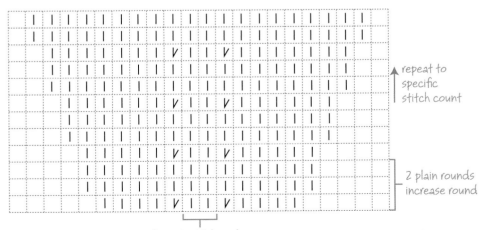

repeat to specific stitch count

2 plain rounds increase round

keep 2 stitches plain

Even More Increases

Increasing in each stitch doubles the number of stitches and quickly adds a lot more knitting. This is another good reason to work the skirt in the round—who really wants to purl across all those stitches?

If you want a fuller flounce, increase in every stitch again on the next row. That will mean a lot more stitches, and your skirt will definitely require more time and more yarn!

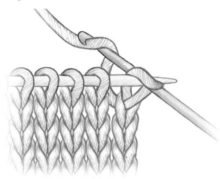

To bind off all those stitches, consider using a comparably sized crochet hook instead of your right-hand needle. Insert the hook knit-wise into the first stitch, hook the yarn, and pull through.

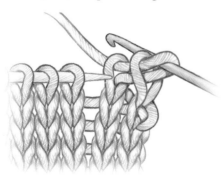

Let the old stitch fall from the needle. Work the same way into the next stitch, but pull the loop through both the stitch on the needle and the loop on the hook. Repeat across the row. Using a crochet hook instead of the needle to "knit" the stitches makes the process much easier.

Creative Options

* Working from the wrong side, use matching thread and sew shiny seed beads at the bottom of the ruffle for weight and sparkle.

* Make the skirt in a soft metallic yarn and a longer length for a dressier look.

* Work the body of the skirt a bit longer and omit the ruffle for a tailored look.

Sideways Striped Sweater

The vertical stripes on this sweater are flattering and stylish. Bands added to the bottom, sleeve, and neck finish the garment nicely. The sweater was designed using sideways construction, working from sleeve cuff across to sleeve cuff in one piece. There are only two underarm seams to finish. Working a sweater this way is not common, but it is easy, and the finished piece looks great.

Finished Size:
34 (38, 42, 46) in./
86 (97, 107, 117) cm
at chest; larger sizes in
parentheses

*Note: While the sweater
was designed to be close-
fitting, allow at least
2–4 in. (5–10cm) of ease.*

**Techniques and
Skills Used:**
Cast on *(p. 19)*, **knit** *(p. 21)*,
purl *(p. 21)*, **bind off** *(p. 22)*,
join new yarn *(p. 22)*,
pick up stitches *(p. 23)*,
weave in ends *(p. 23)*

Finishing:
Seaming *(p. 26)*

Project Gauge:
10 stitches/2 in. (5cm)
over stockinette stitch
18 rows/3¼ in. (8.2cm)
over stripe pattern

*Note: Row gauge is
important for this project
because of the way it's
constructed. A difference
in row gauge can affect
the circumference of the
sweater. Please check your
gauge carefully to make
sure your project is the
correct size.*

Materials:
• **Yarn:** 100% superwash wool
  worsted-weight yarn, 220 yds./201m
  per ball
  2 (3, 3, 4) balls in dark purple (A)
  1 (1, 1, 2) balls in medium pink (B)
  1 (1, 2, 2) balls in light yellow (C)
  1 (2, 2, 3) balls in dark blue (D)
  1 (2, 2, 3) balls in medium orange (E)
• **Knitting needles:** sizes 5 (3.75mm)
  and 7 (4.5mm), or size needed for
  gauge
• **Tapestry or yarn needle**
• **Tape measure**
• **Scissors**

*Note: You will be able to complete some
portions of this design with straight
needles. However, while working the body,
there will be a large number of stitches on
the needle, so a size 7 (4.5mm) circular
needle used as a straight needle may be
more practical.*

Pattern Stitch:
The pattern stitch is simple stockinette
stitch.
• CO 20 stitches with color A.
• **Row 1**: K.
• **Row 2**: P.

Work one stripe pattern segment in
stockinette stitch as follows:
• **Rows 1–6**: Color A.
• **Rows 7–10**: Color B.
• **Rows 11 and 12**: Color C.
• **Rows 13–16**: Color D.
• **Rows 17 and 18**: Color E.
Swatch measures 4 in. (10.2cm) wide
and 3¼ in. (8.2cm) long.

look for a similar smooth worsted yarn of nearly any fiber content. Wool and natural fibers, such as mohair, angora, cashmere, and similar fibers, would work well. Try to pick yarns with some elasticity, because sideways construction tends to stretch a bit. Cottons and linens may not wear as well—the sweater could grow longer as it ages.

The stripe color scheme is based on two dark, two medium, and one light color. Stay with this pattern, but choose your own coordinating colors to create a sweater that expresses your own style.

SWEATER

TIP: Sideways sweaters can stretch lengthwise when worn. This sweater is sized to allow for that lengthening during wear. If you are petite, consider shortening the body length by a few inches. Cast on 5 fewer stitches for each inch (2.5cm) that you want to shorten the body front and back. Work the sleeves as directed.

Right Sleeve
• With larger needles and A, CO 40 stitches.
• Begin working in stockinette stitch and following stripe pattern.
• After working first six rows of segment 1, begin sleeve shaping.

Begin Sleeve Increases at Each Side
• Increase 1 stitch each side, keeping in color stripe pattern and working increases on right (knit) side of work, every right-side row to 80 stitches.

YARN AND SUBSTITUTION INFORMATION:
The yarn chosen for this project is a worsted-weight 100% superwash wool yarn. Yarn label information suggests 5 stitches per inch (2.5cm) with size 7 (4.5mm) needles or 4.5 stitches per in. (2.5cm) with size 8 (5mm) needles. This yarn is well twisted (but not overly twisted) with a smooth surface and no sheen—a good example of a basic worsted-weight yarn. To choose another yarn that would make a good substitution for this project,

Stripe Pattern

Segment 1: A, 6 rows; B, 4 rows; C, 2 rows; D, 4 rows; E, 2 rows.

Segment 2: A, 6 rows; C, 2 rows; D, 4 rows; E, 2 rows; B, 4 rows.

Segment 3: A, 6 rows; E, 2 rows; D, 4 rows; B, 4 rows; C, 2 rows.

Segment 4: A, 6 rows; D, 4 rows; E, 2 rows; B, 4 rows; C, 2 rows.

Repeat these four segments for the entire pattern.

This stripe pattern is repeated from the right sleeve across to the left sleeve. When you finish segment 4, go back to the start of segment 1 unless instructed otherwise.

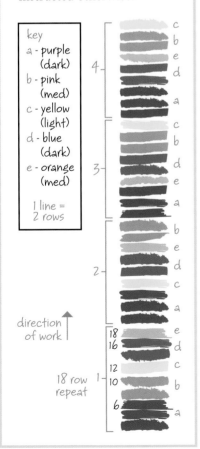

key
a - purple (dark)
b - pink (med)
c - yellow (light)
d - blue (dark)
e - orange (med)

1 line = 2 rows

direction of work

18 row repeat

- Continue in stockinette stitch and stripe pattern until 5 segments are worked, ending with wrong-side row.

Increase for Body

- With right side of work facing you, CO 80 (80, 85, 85) stitches for back.
- Continue in stripe pattern and k across row, including cast-on stitches (160, 160, 165, 165 stitches).
- Transfer full needle to left hand as if to purl.
- CO 80 (80, 85, 85) stitches for front.
- Purl across entire row, including cast-on stitches (240, 240, 250, 250 stitches).
- Continue in stockinette stitch, repeating stripe pattern on 240 (240, 250, 250) stitches.
- Work even for 5 (6, 7½, 7½) in./13 (15, 19, 19) cm, ending with a WS row.

Divide for Neck

- K across 120 (120, 125, 125) stitches; place these stitches (sweater back) on holder.

Yarn Trick

Where are you going to get a holder long enough for all those stitches? You can use a spare circular needle with point protectors on both ends to keep the stitches from slipping. A length of yarn threaded through all the stitches with a yarn needle works too—just be sure to catch every stitch before taking them off the working needle.

TIP: You are now working the fronts and back separately to shape front and back neck. Be sure the stripe pattern is kept in sequence for both halves.

Shape Front Neck

- At neck edge, decrease 2 stitches every RS row 10 (10, 11, 12) times (100, 100, 103, 101 stitches remaining).
- Work one row even.
- At neck edge, increase 2 stitches every RS row 10 (10, 11, 12) times to restore original stitch count, ending at neck edge.
- Place front 120 (120, 125, 125) stitches on holder and break yarn.
- Transfer back stitches to working needles and attach yarn.

Shape Back Neck

- At neck edge, decrease 1 stitch every RS row 5 times (115, 115, 120, 120 stitches remaining).
- Work even to within 9 rows (1⅝ in./4cm) of length of front neck opening.
- At neck edge, increase 1 stitch every RS row 5 times to restore original stitch count, ending at hem with RS row.

Unite Front and Back

- Purl across 120 (120, 125, 125) stitches of back.
- Transfer front stitches to working needle.
- Continue purling across 120 (120, 125, 125) stitches of front to restore original body stitch count (240, 240, 250, 250).
- Work even in stockinette and stripe pattern for 5 (6, 7½, 7½) in./13 (15, 19, 19) cm, ending with WS row.

Bind off Body

- BO 80 (80, 85, 85) stitches of back.

- K across remaining 160 (160, 165, 165) stitches of sleeve and front.
- BO in purl 80 (80, 85, 85) stitches of front, leaving 80 sleeve stitches remaining.

Left Sleeve

- Continuing in stockinette and stripe pattern, decrease 1 stitch each edge every RS to 40 stitches. End stripe pattern at end of segment.
- Work 6 rows in color A.
- BO and weave in ends.

TIP: To reduce the number of ends you will need to work in, carry the yarn up the side when it's not in use. Take care that you don't pull the loose yarn tight when you pick it up again, or the edges will pucker. The yarn can tangle as you work—to avoid this, carefully carry the yarn a few repeats until the tangle is too much, and then cut the ends and start over.

Finishing
Sleeves

- With smaller needle and A, pick up 40 stitches along sleeve ends. Work 1 in. (2.5cm) in garter stitch (k every row). BO and weave in ends.
- Repeat at other sleeve end.

Neck

- With smaller needle and A, CO 90 (90, 92, 98) stitches.
- Work 1½ in. (3.8cm) garter stitch.
- BO leaving a long tail for seaming.
- Sew neck band to neck edge, overlapping fronts.

Hem

- With larger needle and A, pick up 60 (72, 96, 108) stitches evenly along bottom. Work 1½ in. (3.8cm) in garter stitch.
- BO and weave in ends.

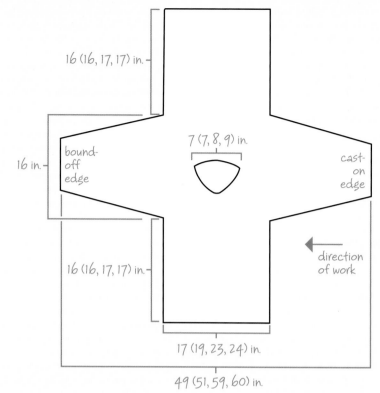

Underarm Seams

- Sew sleeve and body seams, being careful to match color changes. Leave 5 in. (13cm) open at body ends for hem slit.

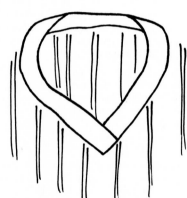

Creative Options

* Your color choices can really spice up or tone down the look of this sweater. Try keeping all the colors in one family, such as an earthy green, for a monochromatic look. Just be sure to use dark, medium, and light values.

* Alternatively, work in a bright hue for one of the stripes—try a dusky green scheme or neutral grays with tomato red for the accent.

* Use metallic yarn for one of the stripes.

* To simplify the sweater and focus on making it correctly, omit the stripes, and make it all in one color.

Projects

For the Home

Sunshine Morning Washcloth

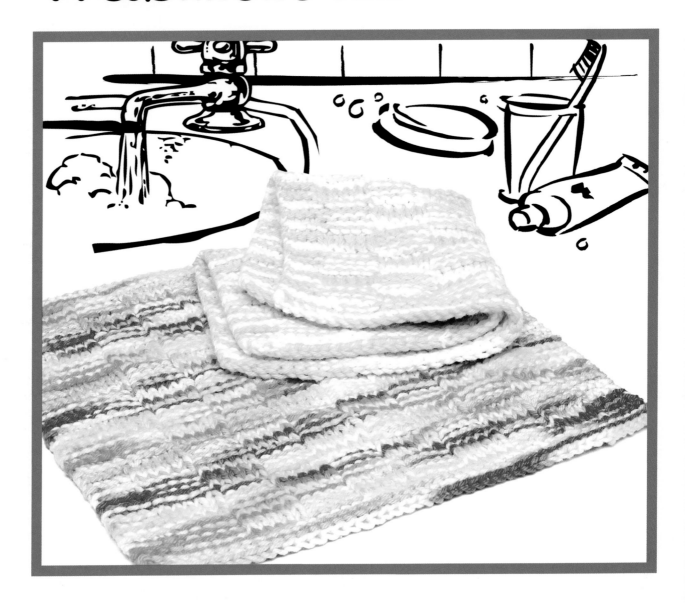

A set of these washcloths is a nice addition to your bath décor, or you can package a set with lavish soaps for a unique and thoughtful gift. The cotton yarn knitted at a sturdy gauge makes the cloth pretty and functional.

Finished Size:
Approximately 10½ in. (27cm) square

Techniques and Skills Used:
Cast on (p. 19), **knit** (p. 21), **purl** (p. 21), **bind off** (p. 22), **weave in ends** (p. 23)

Note: The basic stitches, knit and purl, are used to produce alternating blocks of stockinette and reverse stockinette as well as garter stitch edges. This project calls for no shaping and minimal finishing.

Project Gauge:
20 stitches/4½ in. (4cm) over pattern stitch

Note: Gauge is not critical. It's a washcloth, after all! Just make sure it is knit tightly enough to be useful.

Materials:
- **Yarn:** cotton worsted-weight yarn, 95 yds./87m per skein, 1 skein per cloth
- **Knitting needles:** size 5 (3.75mm) or size needed for gauge
- **Tapestry or yarn needle**
- **Tape measure**
- **Scissors**
- **Steam iron or iron and pressing cloth**

Pattern Stitch for Gauge Swatch:
The pattern stitch is worked over a multiple of 10 stitches.
- CO 20 stitches.
- **Row 1**: K5, p5, repeat to end of row.
- **Rows 2–5**: Repeat row 1.
- **Row 6**: P5, k5, repeat to end of row.
- **Rows 7–10**: Repeat row 6.
- Repeat rows 1–8 for pattern.

Note: The stitch pattern used, alternating blocks of stockinette and reverse stockinette (also called basket weave), is simple but adds lots of texture. It also has the advantages of lying flat and being reversible. The selvedge rows and stitches add a professional finish to the edges.

Mark Your Stitches

Use stitch markers to keep track of the four edge garter stitches. The abbreviations pm (place marker) and sm (slip marker) indicate their use. The markers make it easier to keep track of the selvedge stitches and makes knitting more relaxing.

Creative Options

❋ Make a set of coordinating cloths with matching colors.

❋ Make a bath mat: Cast on 88 stitches, work the pattern repeat a total of eight times, and finish as instructed for the cloth (you will need more yarn).

❋ Use leftover yarn to make small tassels, and tie a tassel to one, or all four, of the corners.

❋ Thread a ribbon on a tapestry needle and weave in and out of the garter stitch border all the way around. Tie the ribbon ends into a pretty bow to finish.

YARN AND SUBSTITUTION INFORMATION

The yarn chosen for this project is a moderately heavy 100% cotton yarn that is not overly crisp. Yarn label information suggests 20 stitches to 4 in. (10cm) on size 7 (4.5mm) needles. It is a moderately twisted yarn and has a slightly fuzzy surface.

Other good choices would be an organic cotton yarn or other natural fiber, such as linen or a cotton/linen blend in worsted weight. Avoid highly spun yarns and those with a mercerized or very shiny finish, as they may not be very absorbent. Synthetic yarns do not soak up water like cotton or linen, and wool is naturally water-repellent.

WASHCLOTH
- CO 48 stitches.
- K4 rows, begin pattern rows.
- **Pattern row 1**: K4, pm, k5, p5, repeat to last four stitches, pm, k4.
- **Pattern rows 2–5**: Repeat row 1, slipping marker.
- **Pattern row 6**: K4, sm, p5, k5, repeat to last four stitches, sm, k4.
- **Pattern rows 7–10**: Repeat row 6.
- Repeat pattern rows 1–10 five more times for a total of six pattern repeats.
- K4 rows, BO.
- Work ends in securely.

TIP: Be sure to work the ends in back and forth across the washcloth so they don't come loose when the cloth is used.

Finishing
- Steam-press and block the cloth for a neat, tidy look.

Felted Pot Holder

These pot holders aren't just handsome—they truly are useful in the kitchen. Felted for durability and to handle heat, the wool yarn also resists moisture. Make a few of these generous-sized holders in different colors to coordinate with your kitchen.

Finished Size: 8 in. (20cm) square	**Materials:** • **Yarn:** 100% wool, worsted-weight yarn, 158 yds./144 m per skein, 1 skein will make two pot holders • **Knitting needles:** size 9 (5.5mm) or size needed for gauge • **Tapestry or yarn needle** • **Tape measure** • **Scissors**
Techniques and Skills Used: **Cast on** *(p. 19)*, **knit** *(p. 21)*, **bind off** *(p. 22)*, **weave in ends** *(p. 23)*	
Finishing: **Felting** *(p. 30)*	**Pattern Stitch for Gauge Swatch:** Garter Stitch: Knit every row.
Project Gauge: **Before felting:** 20 stitches/5½ in. (14cm) in garter stitch *Note: Gauge is not critical, because the finished item will shrink after felting. Just try to make the pre-felting measurements about 11 x 9 in. (28 x 23cm). The pot holder will shrink more widthwise than lengthwise.*	

YARN AND SUBSTITUTION INFORMATION

The yarn chosen for this project is a worsted-weight 100% wool yarn. Yarn label information suggests 16 stitches to 4 in. (10cm) on size 8 (5mm) needles.

The only type of yarn that will produce a suitable finish is 100% wool that has not been treated to be washable. Avoid yarns labeled "superwash."

POT HOLDER

- CO 40 stitches.
- Knit every row for approximately 32 rows or until piece measures 9 in. (23cm).
- BO and work ends in.

TIP: No need to worry about working the ends in too tightly, because they will practically disappear during felting. Trim any remaining ends after felting.

Felting

- Felt *(p. 30)*.

Creative Options

* Work embroidered knots in a contrasting color before felting.

* Add simple embroidery after felting.

* Work a set in stripes of 2–4 rows of each color.

Patterned Accent Pillows

double seed stitch

banded insertion stitch

embossed moss stitch ribbing

These lively pillows will spice up your sofa, chair, or bed. They are easy to make and economical too, so make one or more as housewarming gifts. The stitch patterns are simple but add texture and interest. A pillow is a great project for new knitters.

<table>
<tr><td>

Finished Size:
Approximately 12 in. (30cm) square.

Techniques and Skills Used:
Cast on (p. 19), **knit** (p. 21), **purl** (p. 21), **bind off** (p.22), **weave in ends** (p. 23)

Finishing:
Seaming (p. 26), **adding trims**

</td><td>

Project Gauges:
Pillow 1 (banded insertion stitch) 20 stitches/5¼ in. (13cm) over pattern stitch

Pillow 2 (double seed stitch) 20 stitches/5 in. (13cm) over pattern stitch

Pillow 3 (embossed moss stitch ribbing) 24 stitches/5 in. (13cm) over pattern stitch

</td><td>

Materials:
• **Yarn:** 100% pure merino wool, worsted-weight yarn, 216 yds./198m per skein, kettle-dyed colors: light, medium, and dark orange, 1 skein per pillow
• **Knitting needles:** sizes 7 (4.5mm), 9 (5.5mm), and 11 (8mm) or sizes needed for gauges
• **Pillow insert:** 12 x 12 in. (30 x 30cm), 1 per pillow
• **Decorative tassels:** 2 in. (5cm) long, 4 per pillow
• **Ball fringe trim:** 1⅜ yds./1.3m per pillow
• **Tapestry or yarn needle**
• **Matching sewing thread**
• **Sewing needle**
• **Tape measure**
• **Scissors**

</td></tr>
</table>

Note: While the item is not meant to fit a person, the gauge does matter if you are using a purchased pillow form. Check to be sure! Because knitting is so stretchy and forgiving, the pillows will stretch to fit over the forms and will look better if slightly stretched rather than too big. A gauge that is slightly smaller is better than larger.

Note: The projects as shown used the entire skein of yarn. You may want to purchase extra yarn so you don't run out.

Note: The stitch pattern for the Banded Insertion Stitch Pillow uses two different-sized needles for a novel effect.

Pattern Stitches for Gauge Swatches:
Double Seed Stitch
The pattern stitch is worked over a multiple of 4 stitches on size 9 (5.5mm) needles.
• CO 20 stitches.
• **Rows 1 and 2**: *K2, p2, repeat from * to end of row.
• **Rows 3 and 4**: *P2, k2, repeat from * to end of row.
• Repeat rows 1–4.
Swatch measures 5 in. (13cm) wide.

Banded Insertion Stitch
The pattern stitch is worked on any number of stitches with sizes 7 (4.5mm) and 11 (8mm) needles.
• CO 20 stitches on smaller needles.
• **Rows 1–4**: K.
• **Row 5**: With large needles, k.
• **Row 6**: With large needles, p.

• Repeat rows 1–6 for pattern.
Swatch measures 5¼ in. (13cm) wide.

Embossed Moss Stitch Ribbing
The pattern stitch is worked over a multiple of 7 stitches plus 3 on size 9 (5.5mm) needles.
• CO 24 stitches.
• **Row 1 (RS)**: P3, *k1, p1, k2, p3; repeat from * to end of row.
• **Row 2**: K3, *p2, k1, p1, k3; repeat from * to end of row.
• **Row 3**: P3, *k2, p1, k1, p3; repeat from * to end of row.
• **Row 4**: K3, *p1, k1, p2, k3; repeat from * to end of row.
• Repeat rows 1–4.
Swatch measures 5 in. (13cm) wide.

Sewing Seams

The yarn used to knit the sample pillows is very soft and lightly spun. Be careful when using a yarn like this to sew seams, as the wear and tear of pulling through the fabric can cause it to break. If in doubt, use a matching, but stronger, yarn.

Double Seed

| | knit on right side rows, purl on wrong side rows

— purl on right side rows, knit on wrong side rows

4 row repeat

4 stitch repeat

Embossed Moss Ribbing

| | knit on right side rows, purl on wrong side rows

— purl on right side rows, knit on wrong side rows

4 row repeat

7 stitch repeat

YARN AND SUBSTITUTION INFORMATION

These pillows are made of a 100% merino wool. The yarn is worsted weight and very soft, with little twist to the strand. Yarn label information suggests 4–5 stitches per 1 in. (2.5cm) with needle sizes ranging from 7–9 (4.5–13mm). The low twist gives the strand a soft, fuzzy surface with no shine.

Look for worsted-weight yarns made of wool or synthetic blends for your pillows. Pick smooth yarns to show off the stitch textures best. Avoid strongly variegated colors that could overwhelm the stitch textures. Make a swatch to test your yarn if you're not sure.

PILLOWS
Double Seed Stitch Pillow

- Using size 9 (5.5mm) needles, CO 48 stitches.
- **Rows 1 and 2:** *K2, p2, repeat from * to end of row.
- **Rows 3 and 4:** *P2, k2, repeat from * to end of row.
- Repeat rows 1–4 until piece measures 12 in. (30cm) from beginning.
- BO in pattern and weave in ends.
- Make the other side.

Banded Insertion Stitch Pillow

- With size 7 (4.5mm) needles, CO 46 stitches.
- **Rows 1–4:** K.
- **Row 5:** With size 11 (8mm) needle, k.
- **Row 6:** With size 11 (8mm) needles, p.
- Repeat rows 1–6 for pattern until piece measures 11½ in. (29cm); then work rows 1–4 once more.
- BO and weave in ends.
- Make the other side.

Embossed Moss Stitch Rib Pillow

- Using size 9 (5.5mm) needles, CO 52 stitches.
- **Row 1 (RS):** P3, * k1, p1, k2, p3; repeat from * to end of row.
- **Row 2:** K3, * p2, k1, p1, k3; repeat from * to end of row.
- **Row 3:** P3, * k2, p1, k1, p3; repeat from * to end of row.
- **Row 4:** K3, * p1, k1, p2, k3; repeat from * to end of row.

- Repeat rows 1–4 until piece measures 12 in. (30cm) from beginning.
- BO and work ends in.
- Make the other side.

Finishing (All Styles)

- With wrong sides together, thread yarn needle with yarn and sew back to front along three sides.
- Insert pillow form and sew remaining side closed.

TIP: Be sure the patterns match front-to-back along the seams.

Trim

- Attach decorative tassels, if desired.
- Using sewing thread and needle, sew ball fringe to edge of pillow along seam line with small hand stitches, if desired.

TIP: Start attaching trim at the middle of the bottom edge for a neater finish.

Creative Options

* When it comes to fancy trims, the sky's the limit!

* Try making the banded insertion pillow in stripes. Work rows 1–4 in the first color, and rows 5 and 6 in another for a nice interplay of color and pattern.

Lacy Window Scarf

This window scarf looks much more difficult than it is. The simple lace pattern bordered with garter stitch edges makes a stunning home accent. Finish the scarf with beads or sequins, spangles, or whatever strikes your decorating fancy.

Finished Size:
About 72. x 16 in. (182 x 41cm) after blocking.

Note: This scarf is sized to fit a 36 x 42 in. (1 x 1.17 yard) window. The fabric has a lot of stretch in both directions so the finished size is slightly adjustable. As it is stretched lengthwise, it will become narrower.

Techniques and Skills Used:
Cast on *(p. 19)*, **knit** *(p. 21)*, **purl** *(p. 21)*, **yarn over** *(p. 22)*, **knit 2 together** *(p. 22)*, **bind off** *(p. 22)*, **weave in ends** *(p. 23)*

Finishing:
Blocking *(p. 26)*, **attaching trim**

Project Gauge:
18 stitches/4¾ in. (12cm) over pattern stitch

Note: Gauge is not critical since the window scarf does not have to fit exactly. Make sure the scarf isn't too tightly knit to drape well. If needed, use larger needles to get a nice fabric.

Materials:
- **Yarn:** 100% cotton, sport-weight yarn, 100 yds./91m per ball, 7 balls for scarf as specified
- **Knitting needles:** size 8 (5mm) or size needed for gauge
- **Bead and spangle trim:** 1 yard
- **Sewing thread to match**
- **Sewing needle**
- **Tapestry or yarn needle**
- **Tape measure**
- **Scissors**
- **Steam iron or iron and pressing cloth**
- **Fabric glue (optional)**

Note: You may need more or less yarn for different-sized windows.

Pattern Stitch for Gauge Swatch:
The pattern stitch is worked over a multiple of 2 stitches:
- Using cable cast-on method, CO 20 stitches.
- **Rows 1–3**: K.
- **Row 4**: K2, p to last two stitches, k2 (keep first and last two stitches in garter stitch).
- **Row 5**: K2, *YO, k2tog, repeat from * across, k2.
- **Row 6**: K2, p to last two stitches, k2.
- **Row 7**: K2, *k2tog, YO, repeat from * across, k2.
- **Row 8**: K2, p to last two stitches, k2.
- Repeat rows 5–8 for pattern.
- Knit three rows.
- BO.
Swatch measures 5 in. (13cm) wide.

YARN AND SUBSTITUTION INFORMATION

The yarn for this project is a cotton cabled lightweight yarn. Yarn label information suggests a knit gauge of 17 stitches to 4 in. (10cm) on size 7 (4.5mm) knitting needles. The yarn has a smooth and slightly shiny surface.

To make sure the scarf drapes nicely, choose a lightweight or sport-weight yarn with a moderate to high amount of twist or a cable construction. Cotton is the best choice because it is easy to work with and launder, and it adds body. A cotton blend with linen, rayon, or even acrylic should work well.

Don't choose a heavy or thick yarn, as it may not hang well. Also, yarns with dull or fuzzy surfaces will not show the stitch pattern off well.

SCARF

- Using the cable cast-on, CO 60 stitches.
- K3 rows, begin pattern rows.
- **Pattern row 1:** K2, *YO, k2tog, repeat from * across, k2.
- **Pattern row 2:** K2, p to last two stitches, k2.
- **Pattern row 3:** K2, *k2tog, YO, repeat from * across, k2.
- **Pattern row 4:** K2, p to last two stitches, k2.
- Repeat pattern rows 1–4 until drape measures 72 in. (183cm) or desired length.
- K3 rows.
- BO and weave in ends.

Stitch Chart

| | knit on right side rows, purl on wrong side rows |
| | purl on right side rows, knit on wrong side rows |

| ⊼ | knit 2 together on right side rows, purl 2 together on wrong side rows |
| O | yarn over |

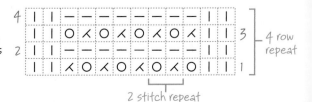

TIP: Don't forget the last YO on row 3! It can be easy to skip, which will result in an ever-shrinking project.

Blocking

- Steam-press scarf on wrong side on a padded surface. Press gently with lots of steam, squaring the edges and pressing along the length of the scarf.
- Allow the scarf to cool and dry completely before moving.

TIP: Press your swatch first to determine the proper setting for your iron, and see how the yarn reacts. Start with the lowest heat setting that produces ample steam. Pressing on a padded surface (like a thick towel) keeps the stitches from being flattened.

Attaching Trim

- With matching sewing thread and sewing needle, sew trim along wrong side of scarf ends, using small hand stitches. Alternatively, you may use fabric glue to attach the trim.

Dealing with Edges

Be sure to join new yarn at the edges, because it more difficult to hide the join in this stitch pattern. Slip the first stitch of each row to help keep the edges firm and neat. To slip a stitch, insert the right needle as if to purl, and transfer it to the right needle without working.

The instructions tell you to keep the two edge stitches in garter stitch. You can use stitch markers to remind you.

Creative Options

* Try repeating pattern rows 1 and 2 for a different lace pattern. Make a swatch to see how you like it.

* Experiment with different trimmings for the ends. Try adding beads, fringe, or tassels. If you have a collection of buttons, show them off at the ends or scatter them over the surface.

* Make a larger version as a coordinating throw. Choose a worsted-weight yarn with appropriate needle size (7–9/4.5–5.5mm), and make as directed.

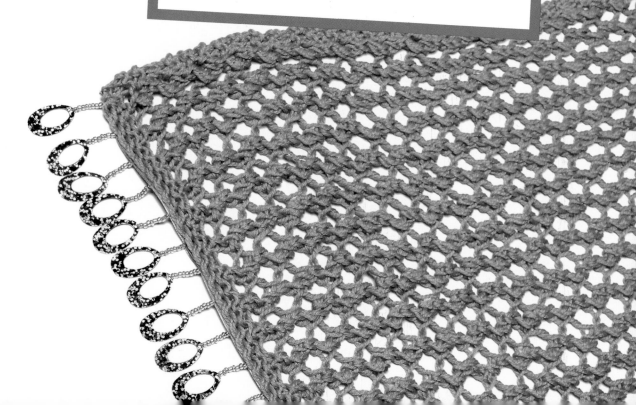

Feather & Fan Throw

This project is an exciting combination of a thick, casual yarn and a lace stitch pattern. The throw is quick to make, and the easy lace pattern looks very impressive. Add personality with your own color choice and trims.

Finished Size: 18 x 30 in. (46 x 76cm) before blocking, 17 x 39 in. (43 x 99cm) after blocking	**Materials:** • **Yarn:** 100% wool heavyweight yarn, 142 yds./130m per skein, hand-dyed colors, 3 skeins per throw • **Knitting needles:** size 11 (8mm) or size needed for gauge • **Tapestry or yarn needle** • **Tape measure** • **Scissors** *Note: The project as shown used all of the yarn. You may want to purchase an extra skein to be sure you won't run out.*
Techniques and Skills Used: **Cast on** (p. 19), **knit** (p. 21), **purl** (p. 21), **yarn over** (p. 22), **knit 2 together** (p. 22), **bind off** (p. 22), **weave in ends** (p. 23)	
Finishing: **Attaching trim**	**Pattern Stitch for Gauge Swatch:** The pattern stitch is worked over a multiple of 18 stitches: • CO 18 stitches. • **Row 1:** K. • **Row 2:** P. • **Row 3:** *(K2tog) 3 times, (yo, k1) 6 times, (k2tog) 3 times; repeat from * across row. • **Row 4:** K. • Repeat rows 1–4 for pattern. Swatch measures 6 in. (15cm) wide, laid flat and slightly stretched. *Note: There are four pattern rows, with only one RS row requiring counted increases and decreases.*
Project Gauge: 18 stitches/6 in. (15cm) over pattern stitch laid flat and slightly stretched *Note: The gauge for a throw is not as important as it is when making a sweater, but your finished item may be a different size if your gauge is off.*	

YARN AND SUBSTITUTION INFORMATION

The yarn chosen for this project is a heavy worsted-weight 100% Peruvian Highland wool yarn. Yarn label information suggests 3.5–4.5 stitches per in. (2.5cm) using needles sizes 8–10 (5–6mm). The yarn is hand dyed and lightly spun with thick-and-thin wool strands. The fuzzy, matte strands vary in diameter.

To choose a similar yarn, look for lightly spun yarns with some color variation and a thick-and-thin construction. Wool is the best choice for this style of yarn, but cotton or a blend with this type of surface texture would work well, too.

Avoid highly textured or furry yarns because they will obscure the lace pattern. If you choose a smooth yarn, the finished look will be different. Thick-and-thin yarns have a casual, even hand-spun look, and they can be knit into great fabrics with lots of interest.

THROW

• CO 76 stitches (includes selvedge stitches).
• **Row 1:** K.
• **Row 2:** K2, p to last two stitches, k2.
• **Row 3:** K2 * (K2tog) 3 times, (yo, k1) 6 times, (k2tog) 3 times; repeat from * across row, k2.

Stitch Chart

	knit on right side rows, purl on wrong side rows
	purl on right side rows, knit on wrong side rows
	knit 2 together on right side rows, purl 2 together on wrong side rows
	yarn over

18 stitch repeat — 4 row repeat

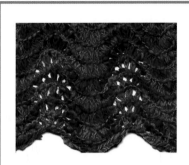

Old Shale

The stitch pattern used here is sometimes called Old Shale. It is a famous Shetland Islands knitting pattern, one of the simplest lace patterns. Because it makes a naturally scalloped edge, it's great for sleeves and hems.

About Selvedges

The instructions call for stitch markers remind you to keep the four edge stitches in garter stitch. The abbreviations pm (place marker) and sm (slip marker) indicate their use. The markers make it easier to keep track of the selvedge stitches, which makes knitting much more relaxing!

Just what is a selvedge stitch? It is a stitch, or several stitches, at the edges of a piece that are worked differently from the body to neaten the edge or to make sewing easier. Also called an edge stitch in some instructions, they are not always included in the pattern stitch counts—check the individual pattern to be sure.

How do you work the selvedge stitches? That depends on their purpose. If the goal is to make an edge neater, firmer, and easier to seam, just slip the first stitch of every row. You will be working the edge stitches only every other row, which tightens the edge. To make a finished edge visually neater, selvedges are often worked in garter stitch.

- **Row 4:** K.
- Repeat rows 1–4 for pattern until piece measures 30 in. (76cm) long.
- End pattern with row 4.
- BO and weave in ends.

Blocking

- Moisten thoroughly with cold water. Roll in a towel and squeeze to remove excess water.
- Align the scallop points to accordion pleat the throw. Using yarn or strong cord, thread through both ends.
- Stretch the throw lengthwise by hanging with a small weight on the cord.
- Dry completely.
- Steam block, if desired.
- Make one tassel for each scallop and attach to ends with yarn and yarn needle.

TIP: Lightly-spun thick-and-thin yarns can be springy and obscure the stitch patterns. Blocking will greatly enhance their appearance.

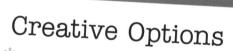

Creative Options

* Use lighter yarn, such as light worsted, and make a shawl.

* Instead of tassels, trim the ends with fringe or purchased trimmings, like bead fringe.

* For a more casual, fun look, choose a plain bulky yarn and work each four-row repeat in the same color to make stripes. Try using team colors to make a great gift for a sports fan.

Projects

Great Gifts

Funky Felted Bowls

Dashing Doggie Coat & Scarf

Cute-as-a-Bug Shrug & Hat

Sizzling Suzy Stuffed Dolly

Handy Needle Case

Funky Felted Bowls

These bowls are an unusual project to felt. They are functional and could hold anything from fruit to nuts to office supplies. The bowls are great gifts, too—just choose the recipient's favorite colors and wait for the reaction!

Pre-felting Dimensions: **Small:** 8½-in. (22cm) diameter **Medium:** 10-in. (25cm) diameter **Large:** 12½-in. (32cm) diameter **Finished Size:** **Small:** 5½-in. (14cm) diameter **Medium:** 7-in. (18cm) diameter **Large:** 8½-in. (22cm) diameter	**Materials:** • **Yarn:** 100% wool worsted-weight yarn, 158 yds./144m per skein, 1 skein for small and medium bowls, 2 skeins for large bowl • **Knitting needles:** size 9 (5.5mm) • **Tapestry or yarn needle** • **Tape measure** • **Scissors**
Techniques and Skills Used: **Cast on** *(p. 19)*, **knit** *(p. 21)*, **increase** *(p. 22)*, **bind off** *(p. 22)*, **weave in ends** *(p. 23)*	**Project Gauge:** **Before felting:** 20 stitches per 5½ in. (14cm) in garter stitch **After felting:** 20 stitches per 4½ in. (11cm) *Note: Because the bowl is felted, the gauge is a suggestion. The finished size will vary.*
Finishing: **Seaming** *(p. 26)*, **felting** *(p. 30)* *Note: The rim of the bowl is attached after the first felting, and the entire object is felted again.*	**Pattern Stitch for Gauge Swatch:** The pattern stitch is plain garter stitch. • CO 20 stitches. • Knit each row for 20 rows, BO. Swatch measures 5½ x 5½ in. (14 x 14cm) before felting. Swatch measures 4 x 4½ in. (10 x 11cm) after felting.

YARN AND SUBSTITUTION INFORMATION

The yarn chosen for this project is a worsted-weight 100% wool yarn. Yarn label information suggests 16 stitches to 4 in. (10cm) on size 8 (5mm) needles.

The only type of yarn that will felt is wool that has not been treated to be washable. Other yarns will not felt properly. Avoid yarns labeled "superwash."

BOWLS
Small Bowl
• CO 8 stitches.
• **Row 1:** K.
• **Row 2:** Increase in each stitch across (16 stitches).
• **Row 3 and all WS (odd) rows:** K.
• **Row 4:** *Increase in first stitch, k1, repeat from * across (24 stitches).
• **Row 6:** *Increase in first stitch, k2, repeat from * across (32 stitches).
• **Row 8:** *Increase in first stitch, k3, repeat from * across (40 stitches).
• **Row 10:** *Increase in first stitch, k4, repeat from * across (48 stitches).
• **Row 12:** *Increase in first stitch, k5, repeat from * across (56 stitches).
• **Row 14:** *Increase in first stitch, k6, repeat from * across (64 stitches).
• **Row 16:** *Increase in first stitch, k7, repeat from * across (72 stitches).
• **Row 18:** *Increase in first stitch, k8, repeat from * across (80 stitches).
• **Row 20:** *Increase in first stitch, k9, repeat from * across (88 stitches).
• **Row 22:** *Increase in first stitch, k10, repeat from * across (96 stitches).

- **Rows 23–27:** K.
- **Row 28:** P.
- BO, leaving a 12-in. (30cm) length of yarn for seaming.

Medium Bowl
- CO 8 stitches.
- **Row 1:** K.
- **Row 2:** Increase in each stitch across (16 stitches).
- **Row 3 and all WS (odd) rows:** K.
- **Row 4:** *Increase in first stitch, k1, repeat from * across (24 stitches).
- **Row 6:** *Increase in first stitch, k2, repeat from * across (32 stitches).
- **Row 8:** *Increase in first stitch, k3, repeat from * across (40 stitches).
- **Row 10:** *Increase in first stitch, k4, repeat from * across (48 stitches).
- **Row 12:** *Increase in first stitch, k5, repeat from * across (56 stitches).
- **Row 14:** *Increase in first stitch, k6, repeat from * across (64 stitches).
- **Row 16:** *Increase in first stitch, k7, repeat from * across (72 stitches).
- **Row 18:** *Increase in first stitch, k8, repeat from * across (80 stitches).

- **Row 20:** *Increase in first stitch, k9, repeat from * across (88 stitches).
- **Row 22:** *Increase in first stitch, k10, repeat from * across (96 stitches).
- **Row 24:** *Increase in first stitch, k11, repeat from * across (104 stitches).
- **Row 26:** *Increase in first stitch, k12, repeat from * across (112 stitches).
- **Row 28:** *Increase in first stitch, k13, repeat from * across (120 stitches).
- **Rows 29–33:** K.
- **Row 34:** P.
- BO, leaving a 12-in. (30cm) length of yarn for seaming.

Large Bowl
- CO 8 stitches.
- **Row 1:** K.
- **Row 2:** Increase in each stitch across (16 stitches).
- **Row 3 and all WS (odd) rows:** K.
- **Row 4:** *Increase in first stitch, k1, repeat from * across (24 stitches).
- **Row 6:** *Increase in first stitch, k2, repeat from * across (32 stitches).
- **Row 8:** *Increase in first stitch, k3, repeat from * across (40 stitches).
- **Row 10:** *Increase in first stitch, k4, repeat from * across (48 stitches).
- **Row 12:** *Increase in first stitch, k5, repeat from * across (56 stitches).
- **Row 14:** *Increase in first stitch, k6, repeat from * across (64 stitches).
- **Row 16:** *Increase in first stitch, k7, repeat from * across (72 stitches).
- **Row 18:** *Increase in first stitch, k8, repeat

from * across (80 stitches).
- **Row 20:** *Increase in first stitch, k9, repeat from * across (88 stitches).
- **Row 22:** *Increase in first stitch, k10, repeat from * across (96 stitches).
- **Row 24:** *Increase in first stitch, k11, repeat from * across (104 stitches).
- **Row 26:** *Increase in first stitch, k12, repeat from * across (112 stitches).
- **Row 28:** *Increase in first stitch, k13, repeat from * across (120 stitches).
- **Row 30:** *Increase in first stitch, k14, repeat from * across (128 stitches).
- **Row 32:** *Increase in first stitch, k15, repeat from * across (136 stitches).
- **Row 34:** *Increase in first stitch, k16, repeat from * across (144 stitches).
- **Row 36:** *Increase in first stitch, k17, repeat from * across (152 stitches).
- **Row 38:** *Increase in first stitch, k18, repeat from * across (160 stitches).
- **Rows 39–43:** K.
- **Row 44:** P.
- BO, leaving a 12-in. (30 cm) length of yarn for seaming.

Finishing
- Thread yarn tail into yarn needle, and sew seam using mattress stitch.
- Stitch around opening at bottom of bowl, and tighten to close.
- Work all ends in.

Felting
- Felt bases.

BOWL SIDES
Small Bowl
- CO 8 stitches.
- Work in garter stitch until piece

Add Yarn for Structure

It may seem like an extra step, but adding the rim and then re-felting the bowls makes them much sturdier. The seam around the base adds stability and structure.

measures 19 in. (49cm), or to fit around circumference of base.
- BO, leaving length of yarn for seaming.

Medium Bowl
- CO 10 stitches.
- Work in garter stitch until piece measures 25 in. (63cm), or to fit around circumference of base.
- BO, leaving length of yarn for seaming.

Large Bowl
- CO 12 stitches.
- Work in garter stitch until piece measures 31 in. (79cm), or to fit around circumference of base.
- BO, leaving length of yarn for seaming.

ALL BOWLS
- Sew ends of rim together.
- Sew rim to base.
- Felt entire bowl again.

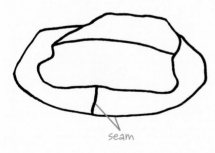

seam

Creative Options

* Add an eye-catching finish to the tops of your bowls with beads, ribbons, and other trims.

* For an interesting patterned look, work both the base and the rim in two-tone stripes. Remember, felting will blur the colors somewhat, so consider using light and dark shades of the same color.

* Use undyed wools and attach organic trims, such as beads and shells, for a natural look.

Dashing Doggie Coat & Scarf

Keep your best friend warm and stylish with this easy-to-make outfit. The instructions include tips for a custom fit for your dog.

Finished Size:
Coat: about 12 in. circumference x 11 in. long (27 x 28cm) to fit smaller breeds, adjustable to fit up to medium-size breeds

Scarf: about 4 x 20 in. (10 x 51cm)

Techniques and Skills Used:
Cast on (p. 19), **knit** (p. 21), **purl** (p. 21), **bind off** (p. 22), **weave in ends** (p. 23)

Finishing:
Seaming (p. 26), **attaching button**

Project Gauge:
18 stitches/4 in. (10cm) over stockinette stitch

Materials:
- **Yarn:** 80% acrylic, 20% wool worsted-weight yarn, 197 yds./180 m per skein, 1 skein for smaller size, 2 skeins for larger sizes
- **Knitting needles:** size 8 (5mm), or size needed for gauge
- **Button:** ½–¾ in.
- **Tapestry or yarn needle**
- **Tape measure**
- **Scissors**

Pattern Stitch for Gauge Swatch:
The pattern stitch is plain stockinette:
- CO 18 stitches.
- **Row 1:** K.
- **Row 2:** P.
- Repeat rows 1 and 2 for length. Swatch measures 4 in. (10cm) wide.

YARN AND SUBSTITUTION INFORMATION

The yarn chosen for this project is a worsted-weight 80% acrylic, 20% wool blend. Yarn label information suggests 18 stitches to 4 in. (10cm) with size 8 (5mm) needles. This yarn is a basic, well-twisted, worsted-weight yarn.

The yarn you choose should be sturdy with a fairly tightly twisted strand. More twist in the strand makes the finished project strong enough to withstand use and snags. Above all, the yarn should be machine washable and dryable.

A superwash wool, blend, or even synthetic in plain worsted weight would make a great choice. Feel free to choose bright colors and variegated yarns to add interest.

Avoid textured and furry yarns. They can snag and will soil easily. Also, they are not generally made for hard use so they may show wear quickly.

COAT
Back
- CO 50 stitches.
- **Rows 1–3:** K.
- **Row 4:** P.
- Continue in stockinette stitch until piece measures 12 in. (30cm) or desired length.
- BO and weave in ends.

Neck Band
- CO 14 stitches.
- **Row 1:** K.
- **Row 2:** P.
- **Rows 3–6:** Repeat rows 1 and 2.
- **Row 7:** P.
- **Row 8:** K.

- **Rows 9–12:** Repeat rows 7 and 8.
- Repeat rows 1–12 until piece measures approximately 7 in. (18cm) or desired length for your dog. End pattern with rows 6 or 12, BO, and work ends in securely.

Stomach Band
- CO 9 stitches.
- Knit across and continue knitting every row until piece measures 3 in. (7.6cm), or 1 in. (2.5cm) shorter than desired length for your dog.
- Make buttonhole: K4, YO, k2tog, k to end.
- Continue in garter stitch for 1 in. (2.5cm).
- BO and weave in ends.

SCARF
- CO 15 stitches.
- Work in garter stitch (knit every row) until piece measures 6 in. (15.2cm) from beginning.

Make Opening
- **1st row:** K5, BO 5, k5.
- **2nd row:** K5, CO 5, k5.

Customize Your Coat
Make a tailor-made jacket for your pup by measuring the length from the base of its tail to the base of its neck. This will be the back length measurement. For the neck band length, measure the distance around the front neck from one back side to the other. Finally, measure your dog's tummy from one side of the back piece to the other, and add 1 in. (2.5cm) for the stomach band length.

- Continue in garter stitch to 18 in. (46cm).
- BO and weave in ends.
- To wear, slip the longer end of scarf through opening and adjust for comfort.

TIP: When binding off a specific number of stitches, count the stitches as you lift them off, not as you work them. The stitch left on the right-hand needle becomes the first stitch of the next set of five.

Finishing

- With RS together, sew short ends of neck band to top sides of back.
- Sew stomach band end to the center of one side of back piece. Sew button to opposite side of back.

TIP: I opted for no fringe on this scarf pattern, as it will only tangle and get in your dog's way.

Creative Options

❋ Make several different outfits to match the weather—warm wool for cold, wet days, lighter blends and even cotton for lighter attire.

❋ Make a matching scarf for yourself:
- CO 30 stitches.
- K every row until piece measures 15 in. (38cm) long.
- Make opening:
- **1st row:** K10, BO 10, k10.
- **2nd row:** K10, CO 10, k10.
- Continue in garter stitch to 45 in. (1.1m).
- BO, and weave in ends.

Cute-as-a-Bug Shrug & Hat

Make this cute-as-can-be shrug and hat in children's sizes in a bright, juicy color. The shrug is easy and stylish, and the hat is whimsical and easy to work in one flat piece. The stitch pattern, alternating blocks of stockinette and reverse stockinette in a pretty check pattern, is simple but has lots of texture.

Finished Size:
3 sizes given:
23 (25, 28) in./58 (63, 71) cm

Note: While the fabric and construction are forgiving, allow at least 2 in. (5cm) of ease for a comfortable fit.

Techniques and Skills Used:
Cast on *(p. 19)*, **knit** *(p. 21)*, **purl** *(p. 21)*, **pick up stitches** *(p. 23)*, **knitting in the round** *(p. 24)*, **bind off** *(p. 22)*, **weave in ends** *(p. 23)*

Finishing:
Seaming *(p. 26)*, **attaching tassels** *(p. 28)*

Project Gauge:
18 stitches/3¼ in. (8.2cm) over pattern stitch with larger needles

Materials:
• **Yarn:** acrylic worsted-weight yarn, 280 yds./256m per skein, 2 (2, 3) skeins
• **Knitting needles:** sizes 5 (3.75mm) and 7 (4.5mm), or size needed for gauge. You also need a short (11 in./28cm) circular needle or set of double-pointed needles in the larger size.
• **Tapestry or yarn needle**
• **Tape measure**
• **Scissors**

Pattern Stitch for Gauge Swatch:
The pattern stitch is worked over a multiple of 4 stitches plus 2:
• With larger needles, CO 18 stitches.
• **Rows 1, 3, and 5**: K2, * p2, k2; repeat from * across row.
• **Rows 2, 4, and 6**: P2, * k2, p2; repeat from * across row.
• **Rows 7, 9, and 11**: P2, * k2, p2; repeat from * across row.
• **Rows 8, 10, and 12**: K2, * p2, k2; repeat from * across row.
• Repeat rows 1–12 for pattern.
Swatch measures 3¼ in. (8.2cm) wide.

Note: This stitch pattern is a variation of double seed stitch, and it makes a nice texture of knit-stitch checks. Each check is two stitches wide and six rows tall.

YARN AND SUBSTITUTION INFORMATION

The yarn chosen for this project is a soft worsted-weight 100% acrylic yarn in a bright, but not harsh, color. Yarn label information suggests 21 stitches to 4 in. (10cm) on size 6 (4mm) needles. It is a moderately twisted yarn with a more prominent wrapping yarn around the main strand.

Pick your yarn carefully when making items for a baby or young child. Yarns that fuzz, like angora and mohair, have loose fibers that can be picked apart and swallowed. Also, stick with machine-washable and dryable yarns that will hold up well to frequent laundering.

To make this outfit, choose a similar worsted-weight yarn with a slightly textured surface. Acrylic or washable wool yarns are a great choice. Cotton is great too, but the finished item may be a bit heavy. Other good choices would be blends of natural and synthetic fibers. Also, be sure that any embellishments are securely attached and child-safe. If in doubt, leave them off.

Stitch Chart

| | knit on right side rows, purl on wrong side rows |
| | purl on right side rows, knit on wrong side rows |

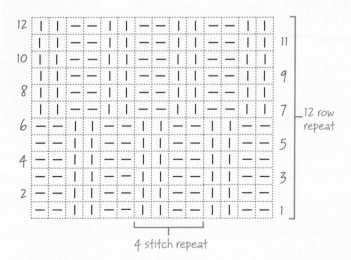

4 stitch repeat

SHRUG
Make Body

- With larger needles, CO 26 (30, 34) stitches.
- **Rows 1, 3, and 5:** K2, * p2, k2; repeat from * across row.
- **Rows 2, 4, and 6:** P2, * k2, p2; repeat from * across row.
- **Rows 7, 9, and 11:** P2, * k2, p2; repeat from * across row.
- **Rows 8, 10, and 12:** K2, * p2, k2; repeat from * across row.
- Repeat rows 1–12 until piece measures 58 (62, 70) in./1.5 (1.6, 1.8) m, ending with row 6 or 12.
- BO in pattern, and weave in ends.

Sew Body

- Sew short ends of rectangle together.
- Fold strip in half with seam in middle of one side. Sew center opening closed, leaving 4½ (5½, 6) in./11 (14, 15) cm at each end open for armholes.

Pick Up and Work Sleeves

- With short circular needles or double-pointed needles in the larger size, pick up 48 (56, 64) stitches.
- Work in k2, p2 ribbing until sleeve measures 6 (8, 9) in./15 (20, 23) cm.
- BO in pattern, and weave in ends.

TIP: To work the sleeves flat, pick up the same number of stitches with an opening at the underarm. Work as directed in ribbing, and then sew the seam.

Hat

- With smaller needles, CO 110 stitches.
- Work in k2, p2 rib for 1½ in. (4cm).
- Change to larger needles and begin pattern:
- **Rows 1, 3, and 5:** K2, * p2, k2; repeat from * across row.
- **Rows 2, 4, and 6:** P2, * k2, p2; repeat from * across row.
- **Rows 7, 9, and 11:** P2, * k2, p2; repeat from * across row.
- **Rows 8, 10, and 12:** K2, * p2, k2; repeat from * across row.
- Repeat rows 1–12 until piece measures 6 in. (15cm) or desired length, ending with row 6 or 12.
- BO in pattern, and weave in ends.
- Fold hat in half with ribbing at bottom and sew side seam, then sew top seam.

Finishing

- Make two 3-in. (7.6cm) long tassels. Attach one to each corner of hat.

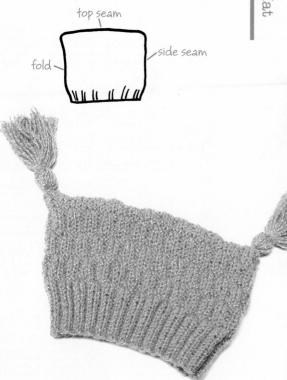

top seam
side seam
fold

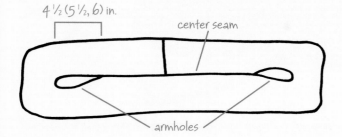

4½ (5½, 6) in.

center seam

armholes

Hat Hint

It looks like you have made a pillowcase with ribbing at the bottom—this is the simplest hat you could make. Just add some trim at the corners and see how cute it is!

Creative Options

* Make several hats and shrugs for a special fashion bug!

* Sew pom-poms or other trims on the hat for fun. Be sure the extra embellishments are securely attached and baby-safe.

* Make an adult version of the hat by casting on 118 stitches and working to approximately 12 in. (30cm) long. Finish as instructed.

Sizzling Suzy Stuffed Dolly

This little pink doll is inspired by primitive folk art. Those popular and highly collectible dolls were homemade and well used. Suzy is easy to make because there is no shaping for the body—it is basically a small pillow with knitted cord arms and legs. Add character and personality with clothes and accessories. Let your dolly express herself!

Finished Size:
Approximately 7 in. (18cm) tall, seated

Techniques and Skills Used:
Cast on *(p. 19)*, **knit** *(p. 21)*, **purl** *(p. 21)*, **knitted cord** *(p. 29)*, **bind off** *(p. 22)*, **weave in ends** *(p. 23)*

Finishing:
Seaming *(p. 26)*, **assembly**

Project Gauge:
20 stitches/4 in. (10cm) over stockinette stitch

Note: Gauge is not critical— it's a toy. Just be sure your gauge is tight enough to hold the stuffing material.

Materials:
- **Yarn:** 50% superfine alpaca, 50% wool light worsted-weight yarn, 219 yds./200m per skein, soft pink solid color for body, 1 skein Leftovers of worsted-weight yarn for clothes, approximately 50 yds. each Dark worsted-weight yarn for hair and face, approximately 5 yds.
- **Knitting needles:** straight and double-pointed needles size 7 (4.5mm) or size needed for gauge
- **Polyester fiberfill**
- **Feather trim, approximately 12 in. (30cm)**
- **Button for top**
- **Sewing thread and needle**
- **Tapestry or yarn needle**
- **Tape measure**
- **Scissors**

Pattern Stitch for Gauge Swatch:
- CO 20 stitches.
- Knit in plain stockinette stitch, alternating k and p. Swatch measures 4 in. (10cm) wide.

YARN AND SUBSTITUTION INFORMATION

The yarn chosen for this project is a light worsted-weight 50% superfine alpaca, 50% wool blend. Yarn label information suggests a gauge of 5 stitches to 1 in. (2.5cm) with size 7 (4.5mm) needles. It is a lightly twisted yarn and has a hairy surface with no sheen.

You can substitute any yarn you like because the finished size of the doll is not as critical as it is for a garment. The color and texture are what give the doll its personality, so choose any yarn your heart desires!

DOLL
Body
- CO 50 stitches.
- **Row 1:** K.
- **Row 2:** P.
- Continue in stockinette stitch, until pieces measures 8 in. (30cm) from beginning.
- BO leaving a 12 in. (30cm) tail for seaming.

Knitted Cord Arms and Legs
- CO 5 stitches.
- K, * slide work to other end of needle, k, repeat from * until cord is 4 in. (10cm) long.

- BO leaving a 6 in. tail for assembly.
- Make 4.

Skirt
- CO 60 stitches.
- **Rows 1–5:** K.
- **Row 6:** *K4, inc 1, repeat from * across (72 stitches).
- **Row 7:** P.
- **Row 8:** K.
- Repeat rows 7 and 8 until piece measures 3½ in. (9cm) from beginning.
- Next row: P.
- BO as if to knit, leave 8 in. (20cm) tail for seaming.
- Sew center back seam with tail, weave in ends.
- Use yarn needle to run a length of yarn through band at top of skirt. Draw up to fit doll and tie a bow.

Top
- CO 48 stitches.
- **Row 1:** K1, p1 across row.
- Continue in k1, p1 rib until piece measures 1½ in. (3.8cm) from beginning.

TIP: Keep the rib pattern for the armhole rows.

- **Armhole row 1:** Work 12 stitches, BO 2 stitches, work 20 stitches, BO 2 stitches, work 12 stitches.
- **Armhole row 2:** Work 12 stitches, CO 2 stitches, work to next armhole, CO 2 stitches, work to end of row.
- Continue in established rib pattern until piece measures 2½ in. (6cm) from beginning.
- BO in pattern, weave in ends.
- Attach feather trim along upper edge of top with sewing thread and needle. Sew button at lower edge of top at front opening.

Finishing

- Fold doll body in half lengthwise, and sew side and top seams.
- Stuff with fiberfill until gently rounded.
- Sew bottom seam closed.
- Sew arms and legs to doll body. Place arms approximately one-third of body length from top. Space legs evenly along bottom.
- Knot tufts of dark yarn along seam at top for hair.
- Embroider Xs for eyes and backstitch curved line for mouth.

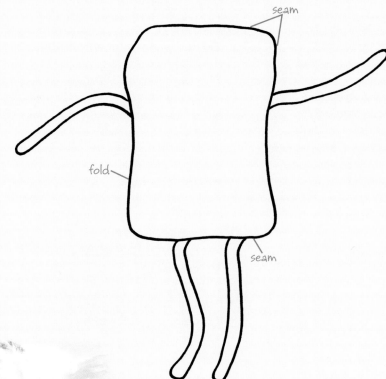

Creative Options

✳ Make whole wardrobe of mix-and-match outfits for your doll.

✳ Embroider a face or use buttons for the doll's eyes. (Don't add buttons if the doll is for a child because the buttons could be a choking hazard.)

✳ Add hair in the color of your choice.

✳ Use different types of yarn, such as a variegated yarn, for the body to make a unique doll.

✳ Try adding purchased embellishments, such as buttons, trims, fringe, sequins, or even glitter.

✳ Make a boy doll by knitting the bottom half of the body and the legs in a different color for pants.

Handy Needle Case

Give a knitting friend the perfect gift—something knitted! After all, who else can truly appreciate the skill and effort you've invested? The case is felted for durability to protect precious knitting needles.

Finished Sizes:
Double-pointed needle case (shown), about 9 x 14 in. (23cm x 36cm), unfolded
Straight needle case, approximately 15 x 18 in. (38 x 46cm), unfolded

Note: Felting is not exact, so dimensions may vary.

Techniques and Skills Used:
Cast on *(p. 19)*, **knit** *(p. 21)*, **purl** *(p. 21)*, **knitted cord** *(p. 29)*, **bind off** *(p. 22)*, **weave in ends** *(p. 23)*

Finishing:
Assembly, attaching knitted cord and trims

Note: Try size 5 perle cotton for assembly. It is available in the needlework section of most stores and comes in a wide range of colors.

Project Gauge:
Before felting: 20 stitches/5½ in. (14cm) stockinette stitch
After felting: 20 stitches/4¾ in. (12cm)

Note: Gauge is not critical. Just be sure your after-felting measurements are close so the case isn't too short for the needles.

Materials:
• **Yarn:** 85% wool, 15% mohair worsted-weight yarn, 190 yds./174m per skein: 1 skein main color for smaller case, 2 skeins main color for larger case, 1 skein in a contrasting color
• **Knitting needles:** straight and double-pointed needles size 10 (6mm) or size needed for gauge
• **Braided elastic to hold needles:** ½ in. (1.3cm) wide: 24 in. (61cm)
• **Hook-and-loop tape:** approximately ½ x 1½ in (1.3 x 3.8cm) for closure
• **Button or other decorative closure**
• **Sewing thread for attaching cord and trims**
• **Strong cord for assembly**
• **Sewing needle**
• **Tapestry or yarn needle**
• **Tape measure**
• **Scissors**

Note: The small double-pointed needle case used the entire skein of yarn. You may want to purchase extra so you don't run out.

Pattern Stitch for Gauge Swatch:
The pattern stitch is plain stockinette stitch with two stitches at the edge worked in garter stitch.
• CO 20 stitches.
• **Row 1 and all RS (odd) rows**: Knit.
• **Row 4**: K2, p16, k2.
• Repeat for length.
Swatch measures 5½ in. (14cm) wide before felting. After felting, it measures 4¾ in. (12cm) wide.

YARN AND SUBSTITUTION INFORMATION

The yarn chosen for this project is heavy worsted-weight 85% wool, 15% mohair yarn. Yarn label information suggests 4.5 stitches per 1 in. (2.5cm) with size 8 (5mm) needles. The yarn is very lightly spun, and the mohair content gives it a pleasantly fuzzy surface.

When choosing yarn for this project, please note that the only type of yarn that will produce a suitable finish is wool or a blend of wools that has not been treated to be washable. Other yarns will not felt properly, so be sure to select one that will felt and avoid yarns labeled "superwash."

NEEDLE CASE

TIP: Instructions are for double-pointed case with straight needle case in parentheses.

• With main color, CO 44 (70) stitches.
• **Row 1 and all RS (odd) rows:** Knit.
• **Row 4:** K2, p40 (66), k2.
• Repeat until piece measures 18 (25) in./46 (63) cm.
• BO and weave in ends.

Strap
• CO 12 stitches.
• **Row 1 and all RS (odd) rows:** Knit.
• **Row 4:** K2, p8, k2.
• Repeat until piece measures 18 (20) in./46 (51) cm.
• BO and weave in ends.

Felting
• Felt.

Make Knitted Cord for Trim

- With contrasting color and double-pointed needles, CO 4 stitches.
- Knit, * slide work to other end of needle, knit, repeat from * until cord is 46 (66) in./1.2 (1.7) m long, or length to fit around perimeter of case.
- BO, and weave in ends.

TIP: The felting process will affect each piece of knitting differently, so test-fit your cord as you work to make sure it is the right length.

Attach Cord to Edge of Knitted Case

- With matching sewing thread and needle, start at center of one long edge and hand-sew knitted cord around edge. Join ends of cord and secure with hand stitches.
- Insert elastic band to hold needles. Fold under one end of elastic and using strong cord, sew securely to center of case at side edge.

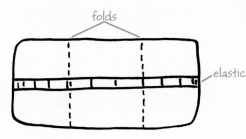

folds

elastic

- Lay elastic lengthwise along center of case, and secure along length at approximately 7-in. (18cm) intervals.

Attach Strap and Closures

- Fold case into thirds, and test-fit strap around center. Trim strap to fit with an overlap of approximately 1½ in. (3.8cm).

- Sew cut end of strap securely to front edge of case. Wrap strap around case, securing to back at one or two points to hold in place.
- Attach hook side of hook-and-loop tape to cut end of strap with matching sewing thread, and sew loop side of tape to strap overlap.
- Attach button or other decorative closure to strap.

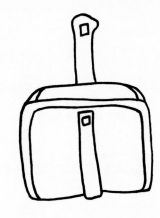

Use the Loops

Attach the loop side of the hook-and-loop tape to the overlap side of the strap. If you attach the hook side, it will be forever snagging on the case when you use it.

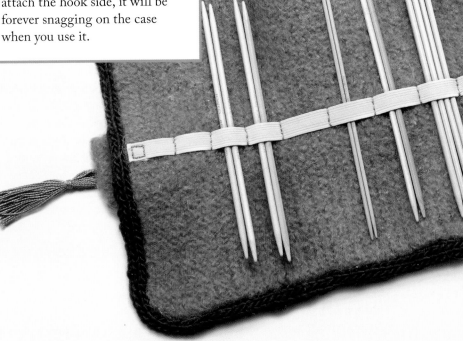

Creative Options

* Make both needle cases in different colors, or add stripes for more interest.

* These cases can be embellished with almost anything—try adding buttons, beads, tassels, or sequins.

Care of Finished Projects

A handmade item deserves proper care to keep it looking good. There are quite a few different ways to properly care for a knitted item. Fortunately, there are also some commonsense guidelines. Use these recommendations, and your projects will be fine.

TIP: Always save the label from the yarn. In addition to all the other great information, it also tells you how to launder and dry the finished item.

Washing

First, there is still a lingering fear of washing a wool sweater. While this stigma may have roots in truth, it is perfectly possible to wash woolens if you are careful. Most labels for wool, blends of wool, and other animal fibers usually specify hand washing or dry cleaning as the methods of care.

To hand wash your precious woolens, you don't have to use your hands and labor over a tub. You can use the washing machine tub to wash and rinse the sweater and spin the water out. The trick is not to let the machine agitate the item or pour the water directly on it.

Remember our felting lessons: Felting is the result of mechanical agitation, heat, and sudden temperature changes. Start with a mild, non-detergent soap. There are quite a few alternatives on the market now for washing woolens. Set the machine for the smallest load and use the delicate cycle. Run warm, not hot, water into the tub and add the soap while it runs. Be sure to use as little soap as possible because too much can be difficult to rinse out. When the water has run in and the machine starts to agitate, turn the machine off.

Gently place your item into the water and carefully squeeze the soapy water through. Do this several times. Set the machine to spin, and spin the water out of the tub. Be sure to stay nearby, as you want to make sure you're there for the rinse.

Stop the machine again at the end of the spin cycle and check that the item is not directly under the water spout. Also, be sure to check that the rinse water is the same temperature as the wash water. As before, gently squeeze the rinse water through the item and spin again. Roll the clean and damp project in a towel and squeeze to remove as much excess water as you can. If you have used the washing machine to spin the water out, there should not be a lot to remove.

Find a moisture-resistant area large enough to hold the flat item. Drying screens are great and should be set up in a well-ventilated area. A good place to dry smaller items is the top of the dryer. Turn them frequently to dry both sides.

Hand washing wool is the same as above, except you have to supply the energy to remove the water that the machine does in the spin cycle. Be certain to squeeze the water out, and do not wring the item.

The occasional label will say "dry-clean only," and you should pay attention. Some of the new specialty yarns may carry this label. Take the care method into consideration before investing the time to make an item. Make sure you understand the care instructions and are willing to follow through with them.

Storage

When your wool items are thoroughly dry, store them carefully. Moths like dark and damp conditions as well as soiled items. Make sure your storage area is dry and all items are clean before putting them away. Using moth repellents is a good idea as well.

Moth repellents range from old-fashioned mothballs to aromatic herbal materials. Be sure whatever you use does not come in contact with the items. Plant materials that work well as moth repellents include rosemary, mint, thyme, cloves, cedar shavings, lavender, and other highly scented plants. You can even use a strong-smelling bar of soap. The key to effective moth repellent is freshness; be sure to inspect and refresh your items periodically.

Never store items without cleaning them. Any residue on the fibers makes them more attractive to moths.

Moths

All animal fibers are susceptible to moth damage unless treated for resistance. The larvae of the moth feed on the proteins in the fibers. If you find moths fluttering around your woolens, take action immediately! Seal the garments in plastic bags and place them in the freezer overnight. Then wash the items and put them back in storage with a moth repellent of your choice.

Resources

Books

The "I Hate to Finish Sweaters" Guide to Finishing Sweaters
by Janet Szabo
A comprehensive guide to all aspects of finishing

Knit & Crochet Combined: Best of Both Worlds
by Monette Satterfield
How to use knit and crochet stitches together to create stylish wearables

The Knitters Book of Finishing Techniques
by Nancie M. Wiseman
An excellent reference for finishing with a range of techniques to produce professional results

Knitters Handbook: A Comprehensive Guide
by Montse Stanley
A detailed reference for advanced and technically curious knitters

Knitting from the Top
by Barbara G. Walker
How to knit nearly any garment (sweaters, skirts, pants and more) from the top down

Knitting Without Tears
by Elizabeth Zimmermann
A knitting classic well worth reading for knitters of all ages and skill levels

Not Tonight Darling, I'm Knitting
by Betsy Hosegood
A fun, quirky, and informative examination of the current knitting craze and past knitting decades

Vogue Knitting: The Ultimate Knitting Book
A comprehensive basic reference book, well worth a place in your personal library

Web sites

Knittersreview.com
Free, online magazine for knitting and fiber enthusiasts; also offers forums and a collection of knitting-themed paper goods and accessories

Knittinghelp.com
A site with more than 150 free knitting videos

Knitty.com
Free web-only magazine with a sense of humor

Learntoknit.com
Online instruction from the Craft Yarn Council of America

Ravelry.com
An online knit and crochet community

Schoolhousepress.com
A great resource for solid needlework education and some wonderful, hard-to-find yarns

Shinydesigns.com
Information and patterns for knitting, crocheting, and other types of needlework

Vogueknitting.com
Fashion-forward knit style ranging from simple to expert

Yarndex.com
A great resource for finding information on specific yarns such as weight, yardage, price, and colors

Yarnstandards.com
Sponsored by the Craft Yarn Council of America, this site collects standard guidelines on yarn weights, pattern levels, pattern sizing and more

MAY – 2010

ACKNOWLEDGMENTS

In working on my second book, I have been utterly amazed at how much I have depended on so many others to help in both large and small ways. It is a huge undertaking to write a book, and I am indebted to everyone who has helped me. There is not enough space or ink to thank everyone who touched this book in some way, but here are the people and companies who must be specially noted:

My husband, who believes in me. Thank you for that belief and for lovingly enduring the process of writing a book.

My wonderful editors, Pat Lantier and Karin Buckingham, both lovely and warm women who encouraged me and answered my questions. Also, everyone at Kalmbach Books, who turns the manuscript into a finished book, must be noted. I am in awe of the effort and result.

Mim Holden, an angel who, as in Knit & Crochet Combined, made the majority of the sample projects in the book. Mim is patient and knowledgeable, and I cannot thank her enough for just being herself.

Carolyn Hawkins for listening, keeping me on track and, most importantly, generously sharing the ideas and creativity that keep me moving forward.

My mother for her understanding of the time required and interest in the process of producing a book.

The yarn companies who graciously and generously provided the yarns used in some of the projects: Cascade Yarns, Classic Elite Yarn Company, Lion Brand Yarn Company, and Malabrigo Yarns. Their contributions and assistance have helped tremendously in making the projects successful.

ABOUT THE AUTHOR

Monette Satterfield is an artist and freelance designer for the arts and crafts industry. She learned to embroider and crochet as a young girl. Learning to knit came later, but she took to it with great enthusiasm. Monette is from Florida, where heavy sweaters aren't worn much, but she still takes great pleasure in designing fashionable knit and crochet projects. She is the author of *Knit & Crochet Combined: Best of Both Worlds.* You can visit her web site at Shinydesigns.com.

Learn to crochet
the easy way

Let's Crochet!, the newest how-to book by Monette Satterfield, is a beginner-level course in crocheting, taking new hobbyists from elementary stitches to an intermediate skill level. Much like *Let's Knit!*, this book presents 20 creative projects for you to build your skills with. Learn how to make a scarf, hat, skirt, camisole, tote bag, and more with detailed instructions and techniques learned in the Basics section. *Let's Crochet!* is a must-have guide for beginners and will appeal to crocheters of all levels.

Available in April 2009

The **beginner's guide** to crocheting

Let's Crochet!
by Monette Satterfield

Start today
with basic techniques
PLUS **20** step-by-step **projects**

62725 • $19.95

NEW! Companion Book to **Let's Knit!**

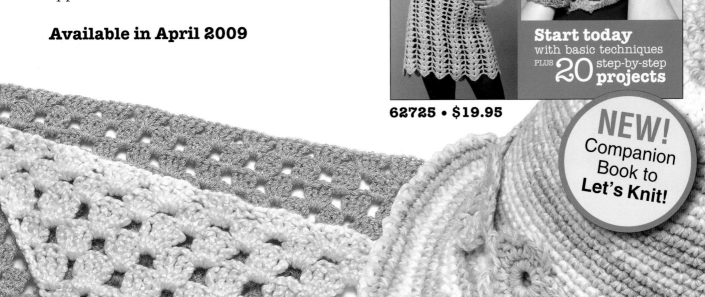

Order online at **www.BeadAndCraftBooks.com** or call **1-800-533-6644**
Monday – Friday 8:30 a.m. – 5:00 p.m. Central Standard Time. Outside the U.S. and Canada, call 262-796-8776 x661.

KALMBACH BOOKS

PMK-BKS-62717P